DRIFTWOOD
from
Popham Sands

Florence R. Oliver

Edited by
Margaret Oliver Ladue &
Edith Florence Oliver

© 2011 Edith F. Oliver

All rights reserved. No part of this publication may be reproduced (except for reviews), stored in a retrieval system, or transmitted in any form by any means, electronic, mechanical, photocopying, recording or otherwise, without the written prior permission of the publisher and/or author.

Cover photograph: © 2011 Kirk M. Rogers, www.kiroastro.com.
Used with permission.

All photographs are from the Oliver family collection
or used with permission.

Custom family tree produced by: Denise R. Larson.

Library of Congress Number: 2011934425

Oliver, Florence R.
Driftwood from Popham Sands/Florence R. Oliver
p. 170
1. History : United States - State & Local - New England
2. Biography & Autobiography : Historical - General
I. Title.

ISBN: 978-1-934949-40-5

Published by:

JWB
Just Write Books

Topsham, ME 04086
Printed in the United States of America

This book is rededicated to my mother, Florence Reed Oliver and my sister, Margaret. Mother wrote this book, Margaret and I began editing and finally it is here in memoriam to both mother and sister who are sorely missed.
Edith F. Oliver, 2011

"This book is dedicated to my late husband, Ernest, and my daughters Margaret and Edith and their families, whose roots are deep in the sands of Popham and who contributed so much to the history and growth of Popham Beach."
Florence Reed Oliver, 1984

Note to Readers

This book was compiled by Florence Oliver from deeds and documents, souvenirs and memorabilia, story times with Uncle Lyme, correspondence and newspaper clippings, photographs and personal recollections to tell the story of life in Popham Beach during the nineteenth and twentieth centuries.

Additional information to clarify historical points and identify sources was added by Margaret and Edith Oliver, Florence's daughters, who assembled the material and edited the manuscript.

Not all the published pieces gathered by Florence during her lifetime can be fully cited. A list of known sources is provided in the Appendix.

Author, Florence R. Oliver

Edith and Margaret Oliver, daughters of Ernest and Florence Oliver. Engagement announcement, December 1962.

History of the Popham Area

For many years, the area around the Kennebec (then known as the Sagadahoc River) was explored before the Popham Colony finally attempted a settlement.

In their exploration of the coast, Hanham and Pring had the assistance of Dahamda, one of Weymouth's captured Native Americans, Rosier's Tahanedo, whom they brought with them and who was found at Pemaquid when the Popham Colony came from England in 1607.

Dahamda, according to *One Man's World* by Jane Stevens, was the name of a hotel on the ridge.

Popham Colony was known in England as Raleigh Gilbert Colony because he brought over the larger of the two boats.

Fort St. George was the first fort in New England, and undoubtedly no more than an "earthwork." A wooden blockhouse was built in 1806 at the fort.

Contents

Note to Readers..iv
History of the Popham Area vi
Acknowledgements..ix
Introduction..xi
Chapter One 1
Chapter Two 36
Chapter Three 78
Chapter Four..89
Chapter Five...111
Chapter Six 118
Chapter Seven 138
Chaper Eight..145
Bits & Pieces 149
   Oliver Family Tree 150
   Resources 151
   Family Pictures...152
   About the Author 155

Driftwood

Drifting fragments of the sea,
Brought by the tide and the ocean's roar,
Are reaped by children in their glee,
As they scamper along the sandy shore.
The western sun is setting,
Across old Atkins Bay.
The same old sun that through the years,
Has seen both smiles and tears.
It throws its rays into the homes,
To brighten the twilight hours.
And the hues in the waters of the bay,
Were never seen in any flower.
Now the long cold days of winter are here,
And the sun creeps away as though in fear.
But soon the increase in the days,
Will bring it back across the bay.
Where Popham folks, both old and young,
Wait for the end of the day.

—Florence Reed Oliver, 1971

Acknowledgements

I am sincerely grateful to the many people who have helped in getting my mother's book published. Without the help of those mentioned and the entire family, I couldn't have done this. This book has taken more time than anticipated, due to the passing of my mother and sister.

I am grateful to have known Nancy E. Randolph for a few years. With her knowledge, expertise and inspiration, this book has been completed the way my mother would have wanted. Denise Larson was also very helpful in the completion of this book in a timely manner.

Margaret Ladue gets my most grateful acknowledgement. She and I took on this project at my mother's passing. My mother's last wishes were to try to get this book published. Margaret took the handwritten notes, and typed them into chapters for the manuscript.

With gratitude I acknowledge Kim Ladue, granddaughter of Florence Oliver, for research she did at the Sagadahoc History & Geneaology Room at Patten Free Library with the research librarian.

I am very grateful to Lynn Reed, niece to my mother, for putting the materials in manuscript form and the support given to me through this process.

I hope you enjoy the stories and pictures of Popham Beach and the Olivers.

Edith Florence Oliver
August 2011

The cover photo of Maine driftwood on Petit Manan Island was provided by Kirk M. Rogers, www.kiroastro.com, with permission.

Matted photograph of Oliver home showing ice cream parlor tent on left, barn to the right and fish house on the shore.

Picnic time at Popham Beach. This great gathering took place on Labor Day, Sept. 2, 1907, on the shore in front of the house of Lyman I. Oliver. Ernest Oliver, Lyman's thirteen-year-old son, is the child between the moustached man and the white hat on the right-hand side of the table.

Introduction

Popham Beach

For many years the area lying south and east as you come down into the big marsh at the head of Atkins Bay along the coast of Midcoast Maine has been known as Popham Beach or Popham, as it is more often called.

Atkins Bay was named for Thomas Atkins who lived on the high hill beyond what was known for years as the Joe Young place, now, Percy's.

Before Popham was officially named Popham Beach, it was called Hunniwell's Point of Beach, named for Ambrose Hunniwell, who bought it from Clark and Lake (Luke) in 1671. During the study of the area in determining the exact location of the Popham Colony, each historian, reaching his own conclusion as to the site, had selected a name of his own choosing.

The name Point Popham was selected by the Reverend William Jenks of Bath (1807). From Honorable Mark L. Hill in 1819 (*Vida Bath Times*. June 3, 1878): "They landed first on Stage Island, and then on Hill's Point, a farm I now own in Phippsburg, on the Kennebec River on the western entrance near the present fort erected by the U.S. Government." The extreme northern end has always been referred to as the Sabino Peninsula. The eastern part rises in steep grades going towards the south and has been known as Sabino Head. In some of Sir Henry Strachey's papers the name Sabino is given as its Indian (Native American) name.

Still another familiar name to this area is Horse Catch Point, referring to the extreme western spur of ledge according to *Sagadahoc Colony* by the Reverend Henry O. Thayer.

In Native American language, *Sagadahoc* means "outpouring water." The Kennebec River was known first as the Sagadahoc as far as Merrymeeting Bay.

Having read a great deal on the exploration and settling of the Kennebec area and having listened to many interesting stories from the older inhabitants, plus what I have observed over the years I have lived at Popham, I have to agree that the Kennebec River once had two mouths, making Popham an island. The following facts seem to prove this:

— Mark. L. Hill refers to the western entrance of the Kennebec River.

— The road out of Popham went from the fort area to Irving Pond (now Silver Lake), then turned westward over the hill following an old Native American trail in the days of the old trading post. This was used even after the road was built across the marsh. Only a wagon track ran along where the road is today and then it was only used in the summer. Many of us have seen the tide over the road at the head of the big marsh on an extra high tide during a storm. Ernest Oliver and Arthur Stevens once paddled a canoe from Atkins Bay through to Campbell's Island creek into Morse's River and Kennebec River and back to Atkins Bay without getting out of the canoe.

Until they raised the road across the marsh in World War II, it was a common sight to see cars held up on an extra high tide. I can remember, before I went to Popham to live, having to remove my shoes and stockings and stand in the water to mark the deepest spot (so a few cars could get across after having been to a dance at Society Hall). I felt like an official road marker.

— In something I read once, it referred to some of the explorers as quoting: "There were high hills to the west of us and Sabino Hill to the east as we came into a 'big bay.'" The hills could have been Morse's Mountain, presuming they came in the western entrance of the Kennebec River.

— From *The Sagadahoc Colony*, "Then in the year 1607 on advancing to explore the river itself—both banks rose gradually in sandy hills. There was no land at all suitable for cultivation but however, it was wooded and well covered with oaks." This could have been Popham and Small Point beaches, also presuming there were two mouths to the river.

— From the Fort Popham Memorial, I quote: "They all went ashore, and they made choice of a place for their plantation at the mouth or entry of the river on the west side (for the river bendeth itself towards the northeast and by east) being almost of an island, of a good bignis(sic), being in a province called by the Native Americans, Sabino, so called of a sagamo or chief commander under the graund bassaba."

Water was one of the first things one thought of when deciding on a place to settle, so it's possible Ambrose Hunniwell built his house near the spring on the bay for that reason. The Reverend Thayer speaks of a depression at the shore line beyond the limits of the so-called fort of the colonists, which wouldn't be far from this spring, presuming he was referring to what was known later as Dark Cove or Duck Cove as some deeds read. I quote: "This formerly was deep and conspicuous and extended back many yards into the area." Opinions of older men and traditions of an uncertain date regard it as the remains of a covered way of a fort that ensued communication with the water (Atkins Bay). If

Driftwood from Popham Sands

Popham wasn't an island at that time, why would the colonists, or the people who lived there afterwards, want to be far from the water except at high tide when it was actually their only means of escape from the Native Americans?

There was always a spring of water on the east side of Atkins Bay, and vessels used to come there and get the water as it kept so good. The Oliver family always kept it dug out as a place for cows to drink when they were out to pasture.

In the last forty-five years I have personally seen a big change in Popham Beach. Many of the oldest cottages are gone and the beach has changed so, one who wasn't really acquainted with it would hardly recognize it. One can just imagine what the sea could have done in three hundred and seventy-seven years. Every year the mouth of Morse's River changes, so it's only likely that a bar built up at the mouth of the western entrance and over the years drift and debris from old wrecks washed ashore and gradually caused dunes along the edge of the beach.

Chapter One

The Olivers

The name "Oliver" is a common name in England, most frequently found in County Durham in the north and in counties Devon and Cornwall (Sagadahoc) in the south.

Lyman Oliver, a native of Georgetown, descended from a long line of David Olivers. He was born April 15, 1808, a son of Thomas and Lucy Sylvester Oliver and in 1812 lived on Stage Island. The family and a number of others fled there to Fort Sagadahoc during a Native American raid. His mother gave birth to a child while they were there.

In 1830, Lyman married Nancy H. Look, a daughter of Samuel and Elizabeth Look, from whom he bought one undivided half of Popham Beach. According to a deed from the 1800s, "The land was bounded as follows: Beginning at a rock South of Thomas Larry's house (Larry's Rock) and running easterly by high water mark and the Kennebec River to the sea, thence southerly by the sea and high water mark to Coffee's River (now Morse's River) thence westerly by Coffee's River and high water mark to head of Campbell Island's creek and property of Captain Rook and north by Atkins Bay to place of beginning."

The other undivided half exchanged hands several times until Robert I. Clark finally came in possession of it. In 1844 Clark deeded to Oliver the following: "A certain tract of land lying on Hunniwell's Point in said Phippsburg, being all that which lies west of a line bearing at high water mark at a large stone near the "Coal Hole" so called, and running southerly by main road and west field fence to the pond (Silver Lake), thence south across the pond to a pitch-pine tree marked, thence south to the sea shore, also one-half of the privilege of an icehouse situated on my land with the privilege of building and occupying another." Received July 29, 1845.

Mr. Oliver married Margaret Irving in 1851. He maintained a small farm and went into the cranberry business on his half of the property. He was a stone mason by trade, and soon after acquiring the property, he started building a house on what was known as Horse Catch Point. It is the oldest house on Popham today.

It took a long time to build a house in those days when you consider there were no lumber yards to visit. An adze, square double bitted axe and saws were about the only tools one had with which to work. The men had to go right into the woods and cut down trees for the sills. The boards all had to be sawn by hand.

Uncle Lyme

Uncle Lyman Irving Oliver, son of Lyman and Margaret Irving Oliver was an experienced boat builder in his day. He designed his own model of a wherry and called it the *Kennebec Wherry*. When asked if he built pea pods he said, "No pea pods, they're apt to put their noses down." The wherry was so named for the pilots at the mouth of the river who used them to go to the ships coming in from the bay to go up river. In those days a captain couldn't enter the river without a license, so he would hire a pilot. He would hoist a flag that meant he wanted a pilot. At one time there was a flag pole on the top of Cox's Head used for that purpose. The *Kennebec Wherry* was built lap strapped which gave it more buoyancy in the rough water.

Along with building boats, Uncle Lyme worked with his brother George building houses and cottages and repairing some, but he preferred boat building. He built many motor boats.

Uncle Lyme, like his English ancestors, was always quoting Bible verses. Over the years, I copied down a few of the most repeated ones, although not all are biblical:

"Behold, I have foretold you all things."
"A man that hath friends must show himself friendly."
"Many are called but few are chosen."
"Let not then your good be evil spoken of."
"As convenient as a cow's tail in fly time."
"As nervous as a long-tailed cat in a room full of rocking chairs."

I never rock in a chair but I think of him.

When a young man, Uncle Lyme took up the hobby of what he called whittling, which was actually doing inlaid wood. We have a couch he started at nineteen years of age. The framework was done in inlaid wood. The point of each star in the pattern was a separate piece of wood. He made many picture frames and boxes. The boxes were about sixteen inches by ten inches. The covers had five hundred separate pieces of wood in them. My daughters each have one. They are really works of art and done completely with common tools—mostly a jack knife. What one could call "Yankee ingenuity."

Uncle Lyme was a member of the first crew of the Hunniwell's Beach Life Saving Station in 1884, having taken his physical exam in November of 1883. He was still a member at the time the sta-

House built by Lyman Oliver. Also home of Lyman Irving Oliver and George A. Oliver and later Ernest W. Oliver. Pictured: (l-r) Mary Butler Oliver, Ernest W. Oliver and Lyman Irving Oliver.

Oliver homestead, Built by Lyman Oliver in 1845 is the oldest remaining house in Popham Beach, Maine.

tion was moved to its present location. The men lived at the station only having time to go home for a change of clothes before returning to duty.

Lyman went to Massachusetts for a while and worked in a shoe shop, but his parents were getting along in years, so he came home to look after them. Soon after the death of his mother in 1890, he married Mary Frances Butler, a daughter of William Butler of The Basin, and had a son, Ernest. (Note: The Basin is currently the Sebasco Estates area.)

When she came to Popham to live, Mary brought with her a white coon cat called Tonkers Jane. One summer Tonkers had a litter of kittens and my husband, Ernest, sold one to some of the cottage folks for five dollars. When it came time to go home, they said they couldn't take the cat and told him they would give him five dollars to board the cat for the winter. Cats in those days lived on milk, scraps and mice. No Puss In Boots cat food, Nine Lives or Tender Vittles in those days.

In the spring Mary and Ernest got word from the people saying they weren't coming back that summer and he could do as he pleased with the cat. He sold it for five dollars. How is that for a cat story?

Uncle Lyme was always looking for spring and dandelion greens. No frozen foods. It was all eaten in season. I used to enjoy hearing Uncle Lyme and his brother speak of the different weather signs. Fireflies meant that mackerel were in the river; a mackerel sky was a sign of a storm; red skies at morn, sailors take warning. He marked on the wall just where the sun would reach on the longest day before it started to go back again.

In the declining years, Uncle Lyme was suffering from rheumatism and didn't get out of the house much. He had a radio and kept up on the news of the day and knew what was going on as

Lyman Irving Oliver   *Ernest W. Oliver*

well as most people. His mind was good until the last, and on a day when the pain wasn't too bad, he enjoyed having company and talking with folks who came to visit him to ask questions and hear his stories.

Dr. Joe Smith of Bath came in once to see Lyme and he told him he had arthritis and gave him some pills to take for the pain. Another doctor said he had rheumatism, so when anyone asked him what his trouble was, he would say, "It's the old-fashioned rheumatism improved."

When someone asked Lyme why he thought he had lived so long, he said he figured it was the way his family ate. Their food was plain and wholesome. The goodness hadn't been taken out.

Florence Oliver

They ate plenty of fish, birds, and vegetables in season. It was a common thing to sit down to breakfast to boiled or warmed over potatoes, salt mackerel and hot biscuits. They always had cows, so there was plenty of milk for chowders and homemade butter. They made sourdough bread as yeast was yet to be readily available.

Uncle George and Uncle Lyme

Uncle George and Uncle Lyme Oliver, as they were affectionately called by all who knew them, were from one of the oldest families that settled at Popham Beach. They also had a sister, Ellen Jane. They were born at Popham, then called Hunniwell's Point, in 1852 to 1855, before the Civil War and the building of Fort Popham, which brought a lot of people there to work.

George and Lyme could remember when there were but six or seven dwelling houses in the village. Most of the people earned their living by fishing and a few by farming. Their father, Lyman Oliver, was a brick and stone mason and was originally from Georgetown.

The first school George and Lyme attended was in their own home. Then they went to school in the old stone barracks that was later torn down when the present fort was built. Then school was held in different homes. Uncle George and Uncle Lyme had weatherproof constitutions and spent all their lives, except for a very short time, at Popham Beach.

Occasionally, Uncle George worked as a water boy at the time they built Fort Popham. The water had to be taken over by a boat, as that part where the fort is located was an island at high tide. By the time he had made the rounds, the supply was exhausted, so it was more or less a continuous job.

Uncle George was an experienced house joiner and as a young man went to Boston to learn the art of building stairs. He could

Driftwood from Popham Sands

put up a stairway in a space where it seemed impossible to erect one. He was an ardent bird hunter and was never as happy as when he was armed with a shot gun, accompanied by his bird dog, jogging along the roads with his old horse, off to one of his favorite cover-ups. There never was a time that there weren't birds hanging up in the shed.

During the Spanish American War, Uncle Lyme helped build the powder magazine to mount guns at Fort Popham and on Mount Desert Island. They both helped build Society Hall. Uncle Lyme took part in several plays put on to make money to pay for building it.

Uncle George was a member of the Life Saving Station as a young man and also went fishing on the Grand Banks. He used to take an old brass spy glass that belonged to his father and an old compass, both of which we still have. Some would say he had a crotchety disposition, but to those who knew him, it was only a front.

In the fall about Thanksgiving time when birds were plentiful, the men and boys of Bay Point and Popham Beach would hold a

L-R: George Oliver, Nat Perkins, Lyman I. Oliver.

shooting contest. Each kind of bird or animal was worth points, and the side receiving the least points had to provide a supper for the winners.

Uncle George Oliver usually came forward with a generous donation of points on this. One year Ernest's donation was a pure black skunk that he had trapped in the sand hills where the state park is today. He didn't know how he was going to get it out of the trap, so he hauled it on his sled to Morse's River and drowned it in the trap. It brought enough points to help make the Popham team the winners. Afterward he sold the pelt for eight dollars—and without having to skin it.

When he was getting on in years, Uncle George would come shuffling across the hall into Lyme's side of the house to sit a while as he could not see as much from his side. Sometimes, he would sit an hour or so and then go back into his side without having spoken hardly a word. Someone asked once if they weren't on speaking terms, yet they were, very much. When asked why they didn't talk to one another, they said, "After having lived with one another over eighty years, there's nothing to talk about."

Uncle George got around the village in his later years more than Uncle Lyme, so he often met people around the store who he hadn't seen for a long time. If they couldn't get to see Uncle Lyme, they always asked for him, and Uncle George would come home and he and Uncle Lyme would sit and talk about the good times they had had with each individual.

Every year when Drs. Tom and George Percy came to Popham during their vacations, they made it a point to visit the brothers. Dr. George would always be quite concerned as to their physical welfare and usually listened to all their aches and discomforts; there were many, and it always ended with several envelopes of pink pills decorating the sideboard. I would have the honor of trying to remember which pills belonged to whom—if I could persuade them to ever take them. Uncle George declared, "Vitamins never did anyone any good, and it was just a good way of throwing your money away." Uncle Lyme figured if a man had lived nearly ninety years without them, what could they possibly do to help?

One would often find Uncle George curled up with his hat pulled over his eyes on the step of the post office with his dog beside him waiting for the arrival of the mail. The young girls would parade around in their shorts and bathing suits just to hear his exclamations. After a while, he would look at his old faithful dog and say, "Come on Buddy, let's go home. This is no place for us." He would uncoil himself from his seat on the steps, grab up his cane and his package of vanity, as he called baker's bread or the modern cereals, and start along the long road home, his unsteady feet scuffing along in the dirt. His aged, stooping shoulders slumped over as he leaned on his sturdy old cane. During the last two or three years of his life, he would rest along the way on a convenient log in the marsh near the road or someone's door step.

Like most New Englanders of their age, they were staunch conservatives in politics, believing entirely in the men and measures on one party and disinterested in others. Over the years, a friend of Uncle George's finally turned his head to the Democratic Party, which always made for a lively discussion when politics were brought up in conversation, as Uncle Lyme remained a staunch Republican.

When George and Lyme passed on, they were greatly missed by the people of the village and the cottage folks who looked forward to seeing them at the daily gatherings at the post office, stores, etc.

Florence Oliver

First Ice Cream Parlor on Popham

Popham's first ice cream parlor was a large tent, with fly, made by Mrs. Lyman I. Oliver on a Sears Roebuck sewing machine, the Minnesota, ordered from the 1902 catalog at a cost of $17 and delivered to the wharf at Popham. I was still using the machine in 1982, and other than a new belt and some oil, there had never been anything done to it. I wonder how many can say that of the machines today?

The ice cream parlor was set up in the field across from the Oliver house overlooking Atkins Bay. The picture of it was taken August 3, 1903.

The picture shows Mrs. Oliver herself on the right and Lizzie Oliver, a neighbor, on the left. Mrs. Oliver was assisted by her son Ernest, who turned the crank to freeze the ice cream and was also the official tester. She usually made two flavors at a time. The old

Ice Cream Parlor in Oliver field, August 3, 1903. Mary Butler Oliver is one of the ladies.

freezer is shown between the two ladies, and in the background is the old cranberry house.

The ice cream was made from real cream from two cows named Daisy and Buttercup. In those days, folks were known to name all their farm animals. Daisy was a wanderer and had to wear a bell, but Buttercup always knew when it was time to go to the barn at night.

Ice cream in large quantities was hard to keep without electricity, which wasn't thought of at Popham in those days. It had to be heavily iced, and during warm weather, it was hard to keep. I suppose that was why the stores didn't bother with it.

The cottage folks used to walk down to the Percy cottage, now the home of Bob Stevens, and walk up through the woods to the Perkins farm (once John Marr's), and continue through Oliver's pasture where Daisy and Buttercup used to graze to the point. The folks would often stop and be refreshed by a dish of ice cream then continue to the village to pick up the mail, do some errands, and return home by the town road or the beach.

People had to depend on what was called "Shank's Mare" in those days, but it enabled them to get around and meet the village folks and enjoy the country side.

Mr. and Mrs. Charles Marsh often made this trip. Mrs. Marsh was a lover of flowers, and they would be loaded down with all the plants, blossoms and sometimes even weeds the pasture and fields offered.

Everybody met the mail boat about noon. It was one of the events of the day. For some it meant the daily paper from home, sending the post cards of Popham scenery to friends and relatives, and picking up or ordering provisions. Eating places, except at the hotels, were out of the question.

The mail boat made an afternoon trip to Bath, and some people would go aboard for the sail and return later in the afternoon.

Florence Oliver

The following came from Emma D. Sewall of Small Point:

The Rivers and Marshes of Small Point (1905)

The Rivers of Small Point and some accounts of the people who in ancient times have lived nearby.

The old documents speak of these rivers (Sprague's and Morse's) as the two salt water creeks going into the land north of Seguin.

Sprague's River

Sprague's River, designated at first only as the most westerly of the two, is called on a map drawn by Phineas Jones in 1731 (now preserved in the rooms of the Maine Historical Society at Portland), Small Point River. It took its present name from the family who owned its western bank for one hundred and fifty years.

When Jethro Sprague settled there in 1762, the creek had no western branch. From the point of rocks west was a beach called the Little Beach. North of it was a fresh water pond and marsh of no use for hay. Sprague dug a ditch through this beach to the pond and tides flowing in soon changed it to a salt marsh. At one time the river swept close to the western end of this beach, making a swimming place for the boys called "Deep Hole." At other times it ran more directly to the sea. An old inhabitant says that the dunes have extended to the west since his childhood and that he has often gathered beach plums on them.

The tides then never flowed close to the end of the bluff, and the country people used to go down the Anderson road and around the bluff to procure salt, which was made at the salt works near the Boston Gunner's Club.

Driftwood from Popham Sands

Near the Point of Rocks, which form the western side of Sprague's River, the settlers of the eighteenth century—the Spragues, the Morses, the Wymans, the Sylvesters and the Lowells—found an old burial place. The Native American Graveyard they called it, but this was an error. It is the burial place of white people of unknown times. It is a flat field of fine old sand extending out into the marsh and quite unlike anything in the vicinity. On a point in this field, there are at this time forty-three graves, marked at the head and feet by rough slate stones, arranged in regular rows and varying in length from that of a tall man to a little child.

Where the people came from is a matter of conjecture. Three sails from a wrecked ship, the *Hanover*, two from a schooner lost off Band Head, and one woman have been laid here within the last sixty years. A rough stone, with the letters S-H-N-V very crudely cut and barely to be deciphered, doubtless marks the resting place of the men from the *Hanover*. If there ever were any letters on the other stones, time has obliterated them. Twenty years ago careful observers say there were twice as many marked graves as can be found at present.

Vandals have removed many of the stones for other use and desecrated some of the graves. Tradition says that Nelson Sprague, an early owner, planted corn over a part of this field. Cleared land was lacking and sentiment must have yielded to necessity. The fact that the early settlers called the place the "Native American Graveyard" shows that it antedated all record. From whence came the people who are buried there? History is mute.

John Drake built on the Sprague farm the first framed house in this part of Phippsburg. His wife, Rachel, daughter of Thomas Atkins, bought this land before her marriage from three Native American proprietors: Blind John, Great Agunicus and Sheepscot John. The house with the deed of the land was burned by the Native Americans in 1676. Mrs. Drake states this in selling the land to the Pejepscot Proprietors. The precise location of this house is uncertain, but some facts have recently come into my possession which lead me to think that it may have been situated in the northern part of the field.

James Sprague, grandson of the original settler, was born on this farm about the year 1800. He ploughed up just south of the Gracy house an old key, nearly a foot long and much eaten by rust, also at the same time pieces of brick. Not far from this place was a very old well. He remembered when it was filled up. His aunt, daughter of Jethro, told him that she had heard that the women used to take their clothes to wash there.

Near this place, by the roadside, still grows a clump of tansy. In olden times this was almost always planted in the dooryard. I believe there is no herb that, once planted, is as persistent in living as tansy. I know of a patch growing in York that even two hundred years later still flourishes.

On the map of Small Point before mentioned, there is a house drawn in the locality called "Hall's House." Hall was probably a squatter as there was no record of his having owned the land. Mr. Sprague's aunt also remembered an old black house that stood somewhere north of the barn and burned down in 1804. When a child, she used to run from the back door of this house down to the split boulder. This may have been the house called Hall's on the map of 1731, and the location that was first chosen and cleared by Drake.

Jethro Sprague of Duxbury settled here in 1762 and built his house of logs with an outdoor cellar in the southern part of the eastern Sprague field, where his well, now overgrown with alders, still remains.

Sprague's River, after the first half mile, became a tortuous line, almost lost in the marsh grass at low tides, but at the highest tides, when combined with a southerly wind, it forms a veritable inland sea, carrying with it the smaller drift stuff of the ocean.

Near the head of this marsh can still be seen the corduroy road of cedar logs laid across by the men who built the road from the fort at Ancient Augusta to the Great Marsh in accordance with a vote of that town in 1718.

A place on the shore of this marsh above the burial ground is called, in the deed to Jethro Sprague, The Old Native American Camp. At the time of its purchase by the Pejepscot Proprietors in 1716, the whole town of Phippsburg was called Small Point, and at the time previous to that, the whole region from Merrymeeting Bay to the ocean and from the Kennebec to Casco was termed Small Point Neck. The best authorities concur in the idea that it received its name from the small point at the southern extremity.

Morse's River

Williamson, speaking of the Popham Colony, says: "They afterward removed to the southeast side of the creek near what is now called Atkins Bay, which stretches into the land half a league and forms a peninsular at the southerly corner of the town of Phippsburg."

This, the nameless creek, has been successively called Atkins, Coffee's and Morse's River.

The marsh it forms is separated from the Great Marsh by Morse's Mountain, a rounded rocky ridge nearly three miles long. Cherry Tree head, its southern extremity, extends to the beach and, just inside it, Morse's River swirls around to the north of a great whitish rock and cuts its way through the sand dunes to the ocean.

About half way up the side of this mountain, and more than a mile from the ocean, there is a beach of sea-washed stones. A geologist says: "It lies at the foot of a cliff, which by the arches and caves-faces shows plainly that it was eroded by sea action."

The tract between Sprague's and Morse's rivers, including Morse's Mountain, was owned before the Native American Wars by John Hanson. After his death, it came into the possession of John Drake and Rachel, his wife, and from them it passed to Oliver Noyes and the Pejepscot Proprietors.

Rachel Atkins must have been a strong-minded woman with business ability. Before her marriage, we find her buying land from the Native Americans, and in all her husband's transactions she appears jointly—"John Drake and Rachel, his wife, daughter of Thomas Atkins." In 1716 we find her again. James Berry and his wife, Rachel, former wife and widow of John Drake, and daughter of Thomas Atkins, sold to the Pejepscot Proprietors a tract of land bounded on the north by a line drawn from Small Point Harbor to the tract one-fourth of a mile wide, extending back into the woods one mile, at the upper end of Atkins Bay, which tract Gregory Mudge had given to said Rachel before her marriage to John Drake. Why he should have given it to a woman, whose father was a landed Proprietor, and who probably owned other land herself at the time, is a question hard to answer.

Daniel Morse, the ancestor of those who now own Morse's Mountain, built a log cabin near the present home of Elijah Morse somewhere about the middle of the eighteenth century. Just at what time is unknown, but it was before the War of the Revolution, for he enlisted and lost an arm in the service. When he returned, his cabin had been burned by the Native Americans. He seems to have had a love for Small Point that was shared by so many people since that day, for after a long time he built another house here and in 1793 took a deed of the mountain and a large tract of land from William Lithgrow. The mountain was then called Mt. Ararat; the river, Coffee's River; and the little mountain Coffee's Mountain. His deed speaks of a bolt in the ledge near the Coffee cellar and this cellar is still plainly to be seen in the field, which is crossed when going to the ruined bridge.

About the time that Morse settled here, a squatter named Joe Wallace had a log cabin halfway up the ridge near the little graveyard, and a man called "Hawker" Blaisdell owned land near the present home of Arnold Morse. From the well, which Blaisdell dug, Mr. Morse still draws his supply of pure water.

Near the head of this river, the eastern branch comes from a pond, which is separated from Atkins Bay only by a narrow rocky ridge. It was on this ridge that Thomas Atkins built his house about 1656. At the time of the Native American Wars, he fled to Massachusetts but returned and is supposed to have died there. The old graveyard on Sprague's River is on land then belonging to his daughter Rachel. Would it be unreasonable to think that they might have chosen it for a common resting place?

On this ridge, also, in 1717 Oliver Noyes, one of the Pejepscot Proprietors and owner of property at Ancient Augusta, built a storehouse. About one hundred years ago John Rourke built the old house that still stands today. Tradition says there was at that time an abandoned house nearby, which was said to be haunted. This may have been the old storehouse.

The pond is called in a deed given in 1656 the Mill Pond. Very early in the nineteenth century it was called Whalen's Pond, from John Whalen, who had a sawmill at its outlet and is said to have carried on a "thriving business." There were probably other mills at this place at previous periods. The name given in 1656 would suggest this. Tradition says that the first one was built by some of the forty-five Popham colonists who did not return to England with the others in 1608. Also there was possibly an early settlement at the south of the river, but of this there is no record.

Again and again, the Native Americans drove the white people away and destroyed their dwellings. This continued until a permanent peace was made.

During the War of 1812 and for years after, there were two places on this river where salt was made, called the Upper and Lower Salt Works. The stones, which were laid to hold the sea water when the tide went out, are still to be seen. The water evaporated by boiling in huge copper pans and kettles.

Eighty years ago there was a long piling wharf inside of Cherry Tree Head, used by the fishing vessels that came here for salt. The grandfather of Mr. Arnold Morse told him that he had seen eighteen vessels in the river at one time.

In 1848 the Morse Brothers launched a schooner of 99.25 tons from the bank of this river—not more than one hundred fifty yards from the home of Arnold Morse. She was named the *Hibernia*; afterwards sold to Honorable William H. Rogers of Bath. She was wrecked in a snowstorm on the shore of Cape Ann.

A few years later they built another smaller craft, called the *Hickory*, about two hundred yards north of the bridge. This sloop was never registered at the Custom House, and her bones are said to rest in Clay Cove near the *Aliquippa*.

Twenty-five years ago, Judge Gilbert made an ineffectual attempt to dam the river by putting stones and brush at its mouth. He thought to redeem a large area of salt marsh and convert it into arable land; but the river broke through the sand dunes, making a new channel for itself east of the old one. The project was abandoned and the salt marsh is increasing. Now the river is deserted. It has been years since a vessel came here for freight or for shelter. At the outlet of the pond, which newcomers call Spirit Pool, may be seen the old stone dam, but of the mill not a vestige remains.

The homes of Arnold and Elijah Morse and a bridge, now unsafe and falling into decay, are all the signs of a man's occupancy that the casual observer will see.

At low water Morse's River runs to the ocean a distance of a mile through the beach and separates the sands of Popham from those of Small Point. It is a stream deep, swift and shelving—yet often low water mark not more than thirty feet wide, and so clear and so shallow that a child might sometimes wade across in safety. It is then a stream so tempting to drive over to reach the opposite beach, when to go by land means a journey of six long mile, that a summer guest seldom hesitates until a great fright someday teaches him what the experiences of others could not. Those who live here call it a treacherous and dangerous spot at its mouth. It is seldom alike on two successive days and has many deep pot holes filled by the last tide with soft sand. One by actual measurement was found to be fourteen feet in depth.

A rock near low water mark, its top almost awash at highest tides, is debatable ground, being sometimes on the Popham sand and sometimes on that of Small Point.

I have known the river to go to the sea one-fourth of a mile west of this rock. I have seen Seawall Beach stretch out so far to the east that I once drove on a sand-spit for nearly a mile southeast of this rock—a trespasser in the domain of Neptune, which I shall never be again. I felt he might rise in his wrath and engulf me.

The Marshes

"Oh! Driftwood fragments sailing in,
Upon the surges of the deep,
God only knows where thou hast been,
What mighty secrets thou dost keep."
Emma Sewall

Florence Oliver

From the Kennebec to Small Point

Years ago, how many no man knoweth, the Kennebec River had two mouths by which it entered the ocean. The river separated at Cox's Head and the Peninsula of Sabino on which the colony of George Popham settled in 1607 must have been an island. Gradually the western arm of the Kennebec River filled with sand. First a bar covered at high tide; then, as the drifting tree trunks and tangled seaweeds caught on it, after long years it became a salt marsh on the river side, while a line of sand dunes fronted the ocean. Among these was an occasional opening, through which in very heavy storms the sea broke and spread its drifting flotsam over the marsh.

From the present mouth of the Kennebec River to Small Point it is now a region of sandy salt marshes, traversed by two narrow salt water rivers, Morse's and Sprague's, and divided by Morse's Mountain, formerly called Mt. Ararat, which comes down to the sea itself. It is skirted by fantastic sand dunes, windblown and wave-washed, in whose bosoms are buried the drift and wreckage of unknown ages—unwritten history, which in all probability will never be revealed. Outside these marshes and sand dunes extend Popham and Small Point beaches—the finest and most picturesque on our coast, while east of the Kennebec, until Sable Island is reached, one hundred miles southeast of Cape Canso, there are no sand dunes and no sandy beaches, if we exclude a very inconsiderable one at the mouth of the river.

I have often wondered why it is that the inhabitants of the seashore are so much more superstitious than those of the mountains. I suppose it must be from the mystery and uncertainty which always surrounds the sea. I do not think it possible that anything inland could inspire the awe that I felt as a child crossing this marsh that filled in the western arm of the Kennebec.

Imagine, if you can, this place. On one side huge sand drifts and dunes and the thundering of the unseen sea; on the other side ruin and desolation, the road itself, a zigzag cart-path in which our wheels cut deep and from which the sand fell as they revolved slowly, winding in and out among the drift stuff and wreckage of every kind. It has been sixty years since I saw it, but I can still see it distinctly. Stumps of giant trees with bleached roots like whitened bones; fragments of masts with rusty irons still attached; the broken stern; a schooner half buried in the sand, its gaping companionway with one door still swinging, showing traces of the light blue paint which had once adorned it; logs with the owner's marks cut on their sides, their ends rounded and battered by the beating of the rocks and rolling in the surf; a piece of broken windlass-slabs; an old deck bucket, made from a cask, with its frayed rope handles; a broken oar, bits of sheathing; parts of a vessel's frame; dangling strips of black kelp; bushes long ago washed from their native earth; seaweeds and shells; everything piled in confusion as the drifting high tides from the river or the heavy surf from the ocean had left it, save where it had been pushed or dragged aside to clear the road. Over all was a wild cloudy sky and howling wind. Little wonder that the effect produced on my childish mind has never been effaced. So strong was it that it filled my thoughts to the exclusion of all else that I should have seen that day. Of the ocean, the beach, the lighthouses and the old, and then abandoned fort, I remember nothing. I have only a vague idea of some time-worn red doors, which I was told opened into the barracks.

Fifty years later I drove over that same place. It is now a graded road, not as formerly a cart path whose approach led through a gate behind an old sea captain's barn. I looked in vain for what I had seen as a child, and I wondered if my memory could have deceived me. I appealed to one of the oldest inhabitants, who confirmed my story. It was, indeed, as I have written, and still by the roadside, buried under the drifting sands and hidden by stunted pines, which half a century has planted, is the stern of the old schooner *Post Boy*. I wonder if its open companionway is still as it was when my eyes gazed on it with awe and I almost feared to see the ghost of the skipper peering out in his sou'wester.

Many years after my journey across this marsh, I undertook with a friend to drive across the marsh behind Small Point Beach. At that time it was little visited except by gunners of the owners of the thatch or marsh hay. It is of a very different character from the Popham Marsh, although I think of equal interest. It is traversed by a narrow winding salt water river, surrounded on three sides by rocky hills and on the fourth by the sand dunes.

The first means of communication between the fishermen and the settlers at the mouth of the Kennebec and Small Point was by a road inside these dunes. It crossed both rivers and could only be used at the lowest tides. This road is now scarcely passable, but, leaving the Small Point road at the Sprague farmhouse, we ventured on it.

Descending a rocky hill, on our left was a piece of stone wall of extreme age—weather-stained and lichen-covered, its lower stones deeply embedded in the soil, in some places apparently held up by the wild hawthorn and black alder bushes, which over long years have grown up beside it. Thrown out of line by the frosts of many winters, it still seems to creep slowly down the hill towards the marsh. After our horse had struggled by this, over huge rocks and deep ruts, through marsh grass and sand, by half-buried legs covered with a tangle of weeds and bushes, we crossed Sprague's River. The depth of this river here at the low tide is anywhere from three inches to two feet as the wind and last night's tides may have left it.

Driftwood from Popham Sands

Coming on to the opposite bank, at first we looked in vain for the road obliterated by each tide, but finally in the distance among the scattered tufts of stiff grass and the purplish clumps of marsh rosemary, we saw the marks of wheels, here and there, full of water. We followed them carefully, feeling like trespassers—so strange and uncanny was it all. On and on they wound, keeping the higher ground close to the dunes or to the huge logs and debris of all kind which had been left at high water, now making a detour to avoid a dark pool, slimy and green, home of the mosquito, and now the huge stump of a tree of a size unknown in modern days, bleached by its long exposure. Large as it was, it had looked so much larger to us in the distance. I looked around almost in fear. We seemed to be "out of humanity's reach." The marsh, its brown grasses and winding salt water river, now at low tide a mere thread, stretched far away to the north till it met the distant spruces. To the south were the sand dunes with an occasional wind-blown stunted pine or clump of bayberry bushes. Near us, skirting a part of the marsh, were the fragments of what in years long passed had been a fence. It seemed to spring from nowhere and to end in that same manner, made of wood gathered from the drift stuff, one end of each branching fantastic stick planted firmly in the sand to withstand the occasional high tides which sweep over it, the other reaching out skeleton arms into space.

Overhead a cloudless sky of intense blue, not a breath of wind to disturb the quiet—only in the distance the muffled unceasing roar of the sea. The solitude and desolation were complete and with a loneliness seldom experienced, we turned back to the haunts of men, feeling almost that we had come back from the netherworld, even though we had left it filled with sunshine instead of shade.

There is comparatively little drift stuff here and seldom a trace of shipwreck or disaster. Yet, into this peaceful spot in the winter

Florence Oliver

of 1849 drifted a part of the broadside of the wrecked ship *Hanover* and the bodies of three of her crew. Of all the wrecks near the mouth of the Kennebec River that of the good ship *Hanover* was the saddest and occasioned the greatest loss of life.

Fifty-seven years ago she sailed from the port of Cadiz with a cargo of salt and willow baskets, bound for her homeport of Bath. About ten o'clock on the morning of October 9, she was seen off Damariscove. Her Captain, George Rogers, was a native of the coast and had been a river pilot. Her mate, Mr. Blethen, was born near the mouth of the Kennebec. From a fisherman's cottage on Small Point his faithful wife, watching for his return, saw the ship with a glass and knew it to be the *Hanover*. The weather was cloudy and threatening, but there was no rain.

Coming into the river the wind suddenly changed, the ship missed stays and drifted on to Pond Island bar, which was that morning one sheet of foam. Just three waves sufficed to break her up, and in an incredibly short time, even before the horrified spectators from the little settlement around the fort could reach the spot, her fragments were strewn on Hunniwell's Point beach—the largest piece being a part of one of her broadsides—while mingled with the smaller stuff were willow baskets all sizes and colors, which had formed a part of the cargo.

The captain's body, dressed ready to go ashore, was recovered and buried from his home in Bath, and the bodies of nine of the crew lie in the little graveyard at Cox's Head. The others drifted that winter into Sprague's River and are buried with the unknown dead in what is known as the old Native American Burying Ground under the Point of Rocks, which comes down into the marsh.

The portions of the wreck, which came ashore at Hunniwell's Point, were burned by a wrecking company for the iron and copper, but the next spring a part of one side of her–about fifty feet long—was found inside the sand dunes near the mouth of Sprague's River. I think this fact was known only to a few fishermen and the few visitors who went there long before the present summer cottages were built. They used to take trips to the wreck to secure relics, such as treenails, bits of copper and the copper nails with which the sheathing was fastened. About twenty-five years ago the sand dunes began to drift over it, and now there is only a mound and a clump of bayberry bushes to mark the spot.

For years I had asked if there were any old wrecks near Small Point, but it was only recently that a young man told me that when a boy, his grandfather had shown him what had always been called a piece of the *Hanover*. I interviewed the old man and he confirmed the story. He said one broadside was missing when the wreckage was burned. The next spring, when the ice broke up on the marshes, this, which corresponded with the lost piece, was found and also the bodies of three sailors, and he added this weird tale.

"They say a little black craft followed close behind in the wake of the *Hanover* as she came past Seguin. I did not see it myself, I had rheumatism that fall; but Deacon John he was a good man and deacon of the church—he lived right in sight of the mouth of the river and he was watching the ship—he saw it, a little black craft following close behind her."

In my ignorance of the superstitions of the sailors and his belief in the supernatural, I shocked the sensibilities of my informer by asking: "And did the little black craft get into the river safely?"

The little old man stepped a little nearer to me and gave a look of pity for my obtuseness. "No," he said, slowly and solemnly, wiping his mouth with his bandana handkerchief, "No, she was never seen again." She was a forerunner. But Deacon John—he told me—he said he saw her. He was a good man and a member of the Baptist Church. (Emma D. Sewall)

Florence Oliver

Seguin Island

One rarely thinks of Popham Beach without thinking of Seguin Island. Like most of the surrounding islands in the river and along the seaboard, in 1790, they were covered with trees. Seguin, having a little hollow in the middle, reminded the mariners of a big saddle. Navigators watched for the island while they were exploring along the coast. By 1849 not a tree remained on it, or on Stage, Salter or Pond Island.

Seguin is one of the oldest settled and most famous islands on the coast of Maine. Ten acres were ceded by Massachusetts to the U.S. government in 1794 and the remainder in 1797.

The act of establishing a lighthouse on Seguin was approved by President George Washington, May 19, 1793, and in 1795 the *Columbian Centinel*, a newspaper published in Boston, advertised for the proposals to build the lighthouse of wood with a stone foundation, and also a keeper's house.

The first light on Seguin was approved by Washington in 1798. It was built of wood and the light tower was 165 feet above sea level. Its lantern was a fixed white light with reflectors that sent the power of light in the ocean direction, the land side being dark.

In the early years, the fog signal was only a bell rung by hand in answer to a signal from a passing ship that was nearing the coast. Later, Congress appropriated $2,500 for a new fog system.

In an account of "Seguin" in a Sunday newspaper dated 1963, when the lighthouse became a bachelor station, a picture showing a century old signal bell that gave way to a modern foghorn was shown. I presume this was the one they rung by hand.

The first keeper was Major John Polerezky of Dresden, Maine, a naturalized citizen of Massachusetts and a veteran of the Revolutionary War. He took charge of the light March 20, 1795.

According to the "History of Dresden," it was when he was on the island that he, in company with Francis Goud, a mariner, and Benjamin Emmons, a merchant of Georgetown, built the schooner *Nancy* on the island. James Goud was her master and she was built for cod fishing.

No doubt Seguin got its name from the Native Americans. I have heard that there is a large crevice in the island, and when the Native Americans saw the water go into the crevice, they said "Sea-go-in," but I'm not sure of this.

In the early 1800s, the light tower began to crumble and Congress immediately ordered a new tower of stone. This lasted about forty years, but the fury of the North Atlantic gales finally swept it into the sea.

During the year of 1853 the board reported that the station needed to be improved, and in 1855 the government made an appropriation of $35,000 for reestablishing the station. In 1859 a fifty-three-foot tower was built of stone and a new Fresnel lens was installed.

Seguin is known as the foggiest light station in the country, and before they had diesel compressors, they had a steam horn or whistle out there. Coal fires were kept banked all the time for the boilers, and the coal was hauled up a hundred and fifty feet to the top of the island with a pair of oxen.

According to an old newspaper article, "Seguin Fog Whistle" — Washington, April 12, 1896: "The lighthouse board notifies mariners that on or about April 30, characteristics of the steam fog whistle at Seguin Light Station at Kennebec River will be changed to a sound during the thick foggy weather, of three blasts of three seconds, separated by silent intervals of fifty seven seconds duration."

Florence Oliver

The only access to the station is a 1,300-foot walkway that leads from the sea to the lighthouse. As the light station's boathouse and landing slip were so far under the hill, a distance of nearly a mile, it made it very difficult in getting the coal to the keeper's dwelling and also to the whistle house. Stores had to be carried this same distance, so a railroad system was installed whereas everything landed could be carried to the reservation in a car drawn up the hill by a hoisting apparatus.

The Coast Guard Station was about a fifteen-minute run, or a distance of three miles from shore to the island. Supplies were delivered about twice a month. Liberty and mail runs were made about twice a week, or weather permitting, the keeper could come ashore in a boat kept on the island.

When the keepers or their families wanted to go off the island,

Popham Beach. Fox Island is in the foreground, Seguin Island in the background.

the Coast Guard's forty-footer or utility boat would take them.

From time to time animals were taken to the island. I have heard tell of a bull calf that was taken out there and he went mad, and they had to shoot him. I often wondered if it was the sound of the bell. When I first went to Popham to live, I often worried about my sanity. I would lie and listen to Perkin's Island bell, then the one at the fort, Pond Island and then Seguin would give that little "grunt" as I called it.

In 1954 kerosene was still being used to fuel the light. It took two and a half gallons a night to run it. Diesel oil was used to run the compressors for the foghorn.

Later, but I am not sure just when, power was installed on the island. The cable, 17,000 feet, runs from Popham Beach to the island, and in some places, when it was taken up, it was buried as deep as eight feet in the sand bar off the beach. It has been down about ten years and should last at least twenty.

The island is equipped with generators and a backup battery system in case of the loss of power. It used this system when the loss of power once lasted about six months.

The currents and tides of the water surrounding Seguin are some of the most treacherous on the Maine coast. Even on calm days there is always a chop on the surface that makes it difficult to land and board passengers.

Sometime in the early sixties a temporary range tower was erected on Seguin for a short time. A special crew was assigned to this task and the material had to be transported by helicopter from the shore on Atkins Bay, now the parking place for Fort Baldwin visitors. A guard was stationed there at all times until the material had gone out to the island.

When the crew arrived they were very much interested in "Sequin Island" as they called it. We informed them as to what they were up

Florence Oliver

against and they agreed when they came off that it wasn't any "sequin."

I found the following poem in a *Youth's Companion* dated December 13, 1900, by Manley H. Pike and I would like to share this with you.

Seguin

She washes her sides in the cross-ripped tides
    At the mouth of the Kennebec;
She's solid rock, 'n' if ever ye knock
    On her ye are safe for a wreck.
She's picked 'n' jagged, 'n' wicked "n' ragged,
    'n' blacker 'n' original sin ---
But it a'most come to bein' to hum
    W'en the Maine man sights Seguin.
Fur she is the mark we hunt in the dark,
    To show us the straight-up path;
'N' the beacon by the day that pints the way
    We wan' to travel to Bath,
There's reefs to stabbard 'n' reefs to labbard,
    Where the offshore currents spin,
But we don't care, ef we see up there,
    The light'ouse the't's on Seguin.
A feller that ain't case-hardened haint
    No business hereaway;
'N' ye will find that that Yankee kin'
    Is the kin' to stick 'n' stay.
Ye don't feel nice, akivered 'ith ice,
    'N' col' 'ithout 'n' 'ithin—
It takes a man to stan' his han'

On a schooner off Seguin.
It blows 'n' blows, 'n' it snows 'n' snows,
   'N' you're blinded 'n' chocked 'n' friz,
Then all the coas' looms up like a ghos'—
Jerusalem!—there she is?
Though ha'f your face is a raw red place,
   The prickles ye like a pin,
He soon thaw out w'en ye hear the shout,
   "Hey, fellows, we've made Seguin!"
We may be rough, 'n' we have to be rough,
   Ez it's nateral to be,
But we do our bes' 'n' we leave the res'
   To the Lord who made the sea.
He's a port aloft we have read it oft,
   'N' w'en we're sailin' in,
We hope we'll sight his harbor light,
   Ez we ust to sight Seguin.

Atkins Bay Bridge

One day as I was looking at an old map of Popham, I noticed on the bottom of the map the words "Proposed Bridge." I asked my father-in-law, Uncle Lyme Oliver, what it meant. He told me that at one time the Popham residents had petitioned for a bridge across the bay. He had forgotten the details over the years, but he told me to look in a box that he kept newspaper clippings in and looked for the one that would explain it.

In 1890 thereabouts, the residents of Popham Beach, under the leadership of P. O. Vickery of Augusta, signed a petition for a bridge across Atkins Bay that would actually save about a three-mile drive for those going in and out of Popham.

The bridge would run between land now owned by Edward DeBery on the Cox's Head Road and Lyman and George Oliver's land on the Popham side.

There were pros and cons to settle between the petitioners before they decided that an iron bridge would be the best all around.

There were many new cottages and hotels being built at Popham at that time, bringing more taxes in to the town, but the words "Iron Bridge" raised havoc among the selectmen and many of the townspeople, for the price of the bridge was going to be high and most of the town wouldn't benefit by it.

As the bridge would be going over tidal waters, it was necessary for an act of legislature, but it was refused in both houses.

Those against the bridge thought the road was good into Popham, probably because they never had any reason to go over it. A good road into Popham never existed until World War II. It was always said among the Popham residents "that it took a war to get us a good road."

This was before automobiles, so a road that a horse and wagon could get over was considered passable. It was no wonder the people relied on their boats and steamboats to get anywhere.

The idea seemed to die a natural death, but the humor of it was carried in a local newspaper and I take the opportunity to share it for it tells the story better than anyone could write it.

Morse's River Bridge

In 1896 the Town of Phippsburg again was confronted with building a road to connect the Small Point Beach and Popham Beach. This entailed the building of two bridges, one across Morse's River and one across Sprague's River. This was petitioned mostly by the cottage owners and people having land to develop.

Driftwood from Popham Sands

View from Percy Cottage 1889. Property now owned by state of Maine. Purchased from the Mathersons.

The following appeared in a local newspaper in May of 1896.

Bridges For Beaches

"Popham sands to be connected with Small Point sand beaches, May 16, 1896. The town fathers of Phippsburg voted with but one dissenting vote, to pay $750, half of the estimated cost of a bridge across Morse's River when the bridge shall be built and passed on as satisfactory to town officials.

This means that the bridge connecting Small Point beaches and Popham beaches will at once be constructed.

The Morse's River Bridge will be built on piling, just north of the "Old Dam" on the Gilbert Marshes. Messrs. Sprague and Hunt will have raised about $900 by subscription along Small Point real estate owners for a second bridge across Sprague River, the location of which will be near and a little north of the Anderson cottage.

When these bridges are built, seaside residents and visitors will have the magnificent beaches of the two resorts for promenading, riding, bathing and hunting. The magnificent sand stretches will then form a continuous beach eight miles long.

According to the newspaper articles, this road caused as much to-do as the iron bridge they wanted across Atkins Bay. After several years of fighting amongst selectmen, county commissioners, and even the Supreme Court, the town was given a year to build the road, which expired and still no road.

Various figures regarding the price of the project were given, ranging from a few thousand to $20,000. Frank W. Carlton, for whom the Kennebec Bridge was named, thought it could be built for $12,000. John H. Stacey of Popham Beach said he knew of somebody who would build it for $4,000. Captain Higgins, the one dissenting council vote, after figuring the length of the bridge and other bridges that would have to be built, estimated the cost would be no less than $9,911. The meeting was adjourned, and I was never able to find anything more in the papers about it. Nevertheless, it was built and my father-in-law, Lyman Oliver, told me they had gone over it many times to go berrying at Small Point. I do not know about the one across Sprague's River. They were long gone before I went to Popham to live, although the road from the town road was passable for those walking on the Popham side. When this road was built, it separated Oliver land in two parts. When we sold the property known as Sand Hills to Mr. and Mrs. L. M. C. Smith for a state park, he closed the road.

Chapter Two

Fort Popham

Fort Popham was built beginning 1861 under the direction of Brigadier General Thomas Lincoln Casey, the engineer who later designed the Washington Monument and the Library of Congress.

It was supposedly built on the site of the so-called George Popham or Fort St. George erected by the 1607 colonist. After it was decided that Popham's Colony was established on Sabino Head at a celebration in 1862 by the Maine Historical Society, it was designated "Fort Popham" at their request.

However, it was not the first fort on this site. In 1743-1744, a breastwork that had been proposed to be built on Arrowsic Island was built at Hunniwell's Point, now Popham. It is supposed that in 1775 fortifications of some kind must have existed, for Arnold's fleet was greeted by soldiers on duty and a pilot was provided for him. In March of 1689, New Town was attacked by Native Americans. The people, forewarned, took refuge in the fort at New Town (Butler's Cove) and in another built at the time of previous wars on Stage Island, which was called Fort Sagadohock.

The fort, which watched the gateway of the Kennebec during the early 1800s was built by the federal government on Hunniwell's Point at a cost of $12,803. The site was that of the present Fort Popham.

Florence Oliver

From Parker McCobb Reed's *History of Bath:* "The Fort was built of brick on a solid ledge, on the extreme of Hunniwell's Point, exactly the site of the present fort. It was mounted with a few cannon of no great consequence, Pond Island being barely within range. Four cannon were taken from this fort and mounted on Cox's Head when a fortification was built there in 1814." In building the fortification on Cox's Head, a large portion of the sods were brought in gondolas from the front of Reed's Neck, taken from the property owned by Colonel Andrew Reed, for which he received no payment. The troops disliked their labor, especially carrying the sods on hand barrows to the top of Cox's Head, which is very steep on the river side.

A man by the name of Clark sold the land for a fort for $15,500. Fort Popham was never finished. Like most forts of the Civil War period, they were outmoded before they were completed. It was built of granite brought from Dix and Fox Islands. The guns that were mounted were given to various towns for historical purposes.

The land that comprises Fort Popham was once an island until the fort was built. The chips from the cut granite were used to fill in the space where the old road went into the fort.

A few years before the new road was built into the fort, we had a bad storm that washed out the road in that particular spot. Ernest took Fred Spinney and myself and one or two others over there to see it. Ernest had never seen it himself but had heard his father tell about it. The chips were in plain sight so there wasn't any way one could deny it.

Modern mine equipment was installed at Popham during World War I to protect the channel to Bath. This was the last improvement made by the United States at Fort Popham.

Fort Popham was garrisoned in 1865-1866, during the Spanish American War in 1898, and also during World Wars I and II.

Driftwood from Popham Sands

During the Spanish American War, Uncle Nat Perkins took charge of building a battery on the right side of the present road leading to the fort. After World War I on January 28, 1924, the state purchased Fort Popham for the sum of $6,600.00.

The house on the left of the picture was later moved to the top of the ledge and it was used for the Sergeants' dwelling.

The first light at the fort was a lantern that hung from a pole about where the lighthouse was erected later. Mr. Llewellyn Oliver Sr. tended the light faithfully for many years. In the 1950s the lighthouse was struck by lightning. Sometime after that the light was put on the top of the fort and the bell was put on the east side of the fort. That was the end of the lighthouse that served for so many years the boats coming in the river.

According to *The Sagadahoc Colony* by the Reverend Henry O. Thayer, Job Lewis built a structure on the site of Ambrose Hunniwell's house and John Marr later built on the same site. This is the place later known as the Perkins' farm and even later the Marsh farm. The state finally bought it and tore down the buildings. It is on the east side of Atkins Bay about half way to the head of the big marsh.

These two houses were the first to have been built after the land was sold to Oliver and Clark. Later Clark sold the point where the fort now stands for $15,500 to the government to build the present Fort Popham.

Many of the first houses at Popham were moved here from Georgetown and they had little or no cellars. Not having the facilities to move the buildings, other than scows, they set them as near the shore as possible.

Most of them were low houses and were used as an ell later when a main part was added. Some that I know were moved to Popham are:

Florence Oliver

Fort Popham at the mouth of the Kennebec River.

    The old Haley house on the corner as you turned to go down to the Coast Guard Station. Fred Spinney owned it last and tore it down and built a garage in its place.

    Uncle Nat Perkin's house, known for years as Marguerite McNulty's home and now Minot Percy's was moved from Georgetown and sits on the edge of the beach about where Spinney's restaurant sets now.

    The ell of the house now Barbara Hyde Bentley's. The part that is there now was built on to the original piece.

    The original part of the home of Camille Dussault, the part being what they used for a garage.

    And the house on the very end of the point at the time Elbridge Oliver's, now Bob Butler's.

    There was one old house that sat right across from Mrs. Mildred Sprague's house, and it was called the Sylvanus Wallace house. I

Driftwood from Popham Sands

Ocean View House, Fort Popham.

Visitors to Fort Popham learned about the history of the fort by reading this wooden signboard, which was erected after World War I but before World War II. From a postcard by Otis N.E. Card of Bath.

Lighthouse keeper's dwelling at Fort Popham before it was torn down. Spring 1965.

Hunnewell's Point and Fort Popham, 1887.

don't know whether that was moved there or not. (Uncle George used to live there). Uncle Lyme Oliver used to build boats in it, the last of its existence.

Before Mr. Lyman Oliver prepared his house so he could live in it, his wife died, leaving a family of five, the youngest a baby of less than two years.

In 1851, he married as his second wife, Margaret Irving, a native of Scotland, who immigrated here with her father and family in the early 1840s. They first lived at Georgetown and then bought the house that Trader Shaw built on Silver Lake. Her father was a rope maker by trade and came from the southern part of Scotland. He went into the hotel and ice business after moving to Popham. A trestle was built from the Irving Pond (Silver Lake) north to Atkins Bay where vessels used to come to load the ice.

Mrs. Oliver was brought up in the rigid Presbyterian faith and was a noted Bible scholar. It was said she had a scripture from the Bible for everything she did. Being fond of gardening, she raised many varieties of herbs and was exceptionally good in treating sickness. The following is a story that her son, Lyme Oliver told me about his mother: "A young mother, having an ailing baby, was told to go over and see Mrs. Oliver and have her look at the child. Mrs. Oliver took one look at the child and said in her Scottish brogue, "he needs meat," meaning the baby was undernourished. The young mother, not understanding Mrs. Oliver, said, "Oh he can't eat meat, he hasn't any teeth!"

A clump of tansy and a hop vine that I had fought for years was still on the grounds when I sold the property in 1976. Also a rose bush that Mrs. Oliver moved outside after finding out it was not an indoor rose can still be found. It flourished there for years. We kept cutting it back thinking it was dead, only to find it coming back better than ever. She died in 1890, so she must have planted

Florence Oliver

the bush out a few years before that. If only some of the bushes we buy today would last as long.

Lyman and Margaret Oliver had three children: George Anthony, Lyman Irving and Ellen Jane (Buell). They were all born in the new house that was unfinished. Lyman Oliver made it his home the whole of his ninety-six years; George, the greater part of his ninety years; and Ernest, the son of Lyman Irving, the whole of his eighty years. Our daughters lived there until they were married in 1963, making a total of four generations that had lived there.

After Lyman Oliver Sr. and his wife died, the place was left undivided to George and Lyman I. Oliver. George built an ell on the west side of the house for himself. The house being what they call a "cape" had a large front hall that ran through the main house. The rooms on the west side of the hall were used by George, and Lyman had the east side. They lived there the rest of their lives.

The house is now about one hundred and thirty years old, and although it has been remodeled inside, the structure of the main house remains the same.

When I first went to Popham to live, I used to complain about the wind, for wind we did have on that point. I often mentioned to Ernest that I thought his grandfather could have picked a less windy spot to build a house. During the last few years, I think I understood his selection of the site and am reminded of the old saying "he who builds his house on the sand…"

Going about by Boat

Boats were about the only means of transportation around Popham at this time. These boats were not the fast outboard motors of today or even the gasoline engines—it meant oars or sails. Uncle Lyme Oliver used to tell the story of how his father, Lyman

Spinney Brothers of Bay Point and Popham Beach. From left: Ernest, Ralph, Herman, Fred and Maurice.

Spinney Brothers of Bay Point and Popham Beach lounging on the Redskin Standing: Morris and Herman; sitting: Ralph, Ernest and Fred.

Oliver, John Marr and Nat Perkins rowed to Portland when he was a young boy and they each bought a lamp and clock.

This was the first lamp that the Oliver children had ever seen. It was late at night when the men folk got home, and the children were all in bed, but Mrs. Oliver was so pleased with the lamp that they lit it and called the children down to see it. Uncle Lyme said it probably looked to them the same as the electric lights looked to us at first. We still have the lamp and the clock, but the clock is not in a very good condition. It runs on weights, and there is only one metal part in its mechanism. There aren't many that work on those today. The lamp has a brass pedestal that sets on a marble base and has a clear glass bowl. I wonder if the clocks and lamps that the other men bought are still in existence.

Another story that Uncle Lyme and Uncle George Oliver used to tell was about a small vessel that came in to Atkins Bay to get out of a storm. It was common courtesy to go out and ask if they needed anything, so when Lyme and George were invited to go aboard, they did so. The cook was Chinese and he had a yellow cat for a mascot. The boys were quite taken with the cat; it was the first they had ever seen of that color. Neither of them ever said how the cat got off the ship, but after they returned ashore, the cat appeared from nowhere and ever after a yellow cat was called a Popham cat.

George Popham Memorial

Believing that Fort Popham was on the site of the Popham Colony's Fort St. George, the Maine Historical Society had received permission from the government to place a memorial stone in the walls of the fort with a suitable inscription relative to the founding of the Popham Colony.

Driftwood from Popham Sands

At the celebration of the colony in 1862, services were held in connection with the memorial but the stone wasn't set, possibly due to the fact that the walls were not ready for it.

During the Civil War, it was learned that Fort Popham was inadequate as a defense to the river, so the fort was never finished. The block of granite on which the inscription was made was left boxed until 1907.

By then, research had proved that the fort of the colonists was not on the site of the present Fort Popham, so in June of 1906 the Maine Historical Society was granted permission to request the transfer of the stone to the recently identified site of Fort St. George on Sabino Head. The War Department donated a piece of stone for a base to place the memorial prepared in 1862 in a new form. The wording was changed from "The first colony" to "The first English colony on the shores of New England" and a change from Old Style to New was cut as follows:

The First English Colony
On the shores of New England
Was founded here
August 20, N.S. 1607
Under
George Popham

From our house we could hear people talking from the area and it used to amuse us to hear someone say, "Do you suppose he was actually buried under that stone?"

What is supposed to have been the site of the Popham Colony is now the site of Fort Baldwin. At that time it belonged to the government, so permission was obtained by the Secretary of War to put the marker on government land, but a sightly location could not be found, so permission was given by Uncle George and Uncle Lyme Oliver to put the memorial on their land, where it

Florence Oliver

still remains, overlooking the mouth of the river, Atkins Bay and Fort Popham, with the idea that if the property was ever sold, the monument went with it.

During the time the Maine Historical Society was trying to determine the exact location of the George Popham Colony site, there was much running around with maps, tramping the grass in the field and asking foolish questions, according to Uncle George and Uncle Lyme Oliver. Being well along in years and not having the knowledge of the subject as we have today, they were not too interested in the project and not too pleased at having their hay trampled.

One day while talking to the historical society people, Uncle George told them he was more than glad to hear that they had decided on something definite. Finally, Uncle Lyme asked them

"Monument on Sabine Hill, erected by Maine Historical Society, and inscribed as follows, 'The First English Colony on the Shores of New England was Founded Here August 20, 1607, under George Popham.'" From a postcard by Geo. S. Graves.

why they wanted to put the marker up on that ledge.

"According to the records we have from over across," one man said, "we believe that is the spot where George Popham had his fort and where he lived and died." Uncle Lyme looked at him with his steely blue eyes and said, "What did he die of?" The gentleman said, "Oh we don't know that! All we know is that he died there in the month of February." Uncle Lyme looked up in his easy going manner and remarked. "I do." "You do?" the gentleman asked? Uncle Lyme replied with a chuckle, "If he lived up on that ledge and died in the month of February, he froze to death."

Popham's Cannon

The cannon that sits on the river beach overlooking the mouth of the river was mounted in Fort Popham during the Civil War. According to the government, these cannon are known as Parrot Rifles, and when the war was over, they were given to civil organizations, museums, etc., on request.

In the fall of 1904, twenty-one residents of Popham Beach signed a petition asking for one of the cannons to be donated to the village. At that time the only cannon available for donation were located too far away to obtain them for Popham, but in January of 1905 they received a letter from Washington, D.C. informing them that the commander of Bath, Maine, G.A.R. post had declined to accept the gun offered the post, and Washington would be glad to turn it over to the residents of Popham Beach with information as "to whom this gun shall be turned over."

On January 24, 1905, from a letter to Sergeant James Richardson, in charge of Fort Popham: "I am instructed by the Chief of Ordnance to inform you that the Sedgewick Post of Bath, Maine, has declined to remove the rifle from the post and to direct that

Florence Oliver

This house sat on the former site of Fort St. George. It was called the State House by local residents. It was razed in the late 1960s. Some Oliver family members lived there during the 1940s.

you turn over this rifle, under the same conditions mentioned in the letter of August 7, 1902, to Mr. J.H. Stacey Popham Beach, Maine for the Village of Popham Beach."

Previous to the town meeting of 1964, when the town reports had been delivered, there was an article in the warrant asking what sum of money the town would raise for upkeep of the cannon at Popham. Immediately, the question of its ownership was brought up, and because ownership couldn't be proved, nobody would believe that the cannon had been given to the people of Popham Beach. Previously, in most cases, towns had been the recipients of such gifts, but that wasn't so in this case.

It ended with Colonel Joe A. Bennett, a selectman of the town, making a motion to dismiss the article until such time as proof

15-inch guns, Fort Popham, 1887.

of ownership would be found. He immediately on his own took numbers, etc., from the cannon and corresponded to the Department of the Army at the Pentagon.

At the annual meeting of the Phippsburg Historical Society that summer, Colonel Bennett showed his Military History of Phippsburg slides of the cannon and the petition and letters regarding the cannon that he received from the War Department. The subject of the cannon was dropped like "a hot potato." However, it did provide the *Observer* with several columns of humor as to where the cannon would end up—on someone's lawn, inside Fort Popham, or on some scrap heap.

Commander Walter Raleigh Gilbert

In the fall of 1961, Commander Walter Raleigh Gilbert, a ninth generation direct descendant of Captain Raleigh Gilbert, took several samples of leaf seeds from the site of the George Popham

One of the forty-two cannon at Fort Popham.

Memorial and planted them at Compton Castle where he resides.

In a letter dated November 12, 1963, from Charles P. Bradford, Superintendent of Historic Sites to Ernest Oliver, "Commander Gilbert says in his last letter that he forgot to show me when I was there, the four or five bushes now five or six feet tall, which he has raised from the leaf seeds right near the plaque of the Popham Colony. In your own judgment, Ernest, what kind of tree is he referring to?"

Popham Colony-Gilbert Plaque

From *The Times Record*, August 20, 1975:

Members of the Maine Society, Daughters of the American Colonists and special guests held a proxy marking a plaque presentation ceremony at Popham, Tuesday at the site of the 1607-08 Popham Colony.

The plaque, which commemorates Captain Raleigh Gilbert, one of the leaders of the colony, will be sent this fall to his native home at Compton Castle, South Devon, England. Commander Walter Raleigh Gilbert, a ninth generation descendant of the colony captain, lives at the castle.

The plaque was designed and executed by Artist Jay Hanna of Rockport.

Charles P. Bradford of The Nature Conservancy, formerly with the State Park Recreation Department, made the presentation of the Popham Colony-Gilbert plaque. The Park's Historic Sites Advisory Commission officially identified the colony site for the State of Maine in 1965.

Among the honored guests were, Mrs. Ernest Oliver of Popham whose house is on part of the Popham Colony site, Mrs. Gail Roberts, Phippsburg second selectman, Mrs. Betty Herron, a native of London, now a U.S. citizen and Phippsburg Town Clerk. Mrs. Thomas Fairchild, state regent of the Daughters of the Colonies read a cablegram from Commander Walter Raleigh Gilbert who referred to the historical event as "another valued link across the seas and centuries."

United States Life Saving Station

Up until 1875 there was no protection for boats of any kind at the mouth of the Kennebec River. Eventually the government saw a great need for a life saving station there. The Secretary of the Treasury was authorized by law to establish a Life Saving Station by Congress by act of March 3, 1875, provided as follows: "The Secretary of the Treasury is hereby authorized, whenever he shall deem it advisable to acquire, by donation or purchase, in behalf of the U.S., the right to use and occupy sites for Life Saving or Lifeboat Stations Houses of Refuge and sites for overhead beacons, the establishment of which has been, or shall hereafter be, authorized by Congress."

However it was not until July 9, 1883, that a deed in consideration of one dollar was signed between the Fort Popham Summer Resort Association of Augusta, Maine, of the first part and the United States represented by the Secretary of the Treasury, party of the second part. The lot was described as bounded as follows: Beginning at a point bearing west fifteen degrees south from lower Sugar Loaf, so called, and north 30 degrees west from Pond Island Light House running east 150 feet, thence south 150 feet, thence west 150 feet thence north to first mentioned bound, be the contents what they may and with full rights of egress and ingress-thereto in a direction over other lands of the granter by these in the employ of the U.S. on foot or with vehicles of any kind, with boats or any articles used for the purpose of carrying out the intentions of Congress in providing for the establishment of Life Saving Stations, and the right to pass over any lands of the granter in any manner in the prosecution of said purpose. And also the right to erect such structures upon the said land as the U.S. may see fit, and to remove any and all such structures and appliances at any time; the said premises to be used and occupied for the purpose named in said act of March 3, 1875. In witness whereof, the parties hereto have set their hands and seals this ninth day of July A.D. 1883.

On January 14, 1884 under John H. Haley for fifty dollars a month or three dollars a day for the active season, the following were signed up:

Driftwood from Popham Sands

U.S. Life Saving Station, 1887, on original site before it was moved in 1889.

Life Saving Station, lifeboat and crew, Kennebec River, Popham Beach.

First site of Hunnewell's Beach Life Saving Station (right of picture).

Florence Oliver

Coast Guard Station and boat house at Popham. Annie Stacey third house on left.

Hunnewell's Beach Life Saving Station and crew.

Driftwood from Popham Sands

Coast Guard lifeboat at mouth of the Kennebec River.

Captain Zina Spinney at Popham Beach Life Saving Station.

Byron M. Oliver	Pilot	Age 35	
Elijah A. Morse	Seaman	Age 34	Small Point
Bradbury P. Todd	Pilot	Age 42	Georgetown
Thomas R. Marr	Seamen	Age 46	Popham Beach
Warren Davis	Fisherman	Age 37	
Lyman I. Oliver	Fisherman	Age 29	Popham Beach
Cyrus L. Oliver	Fisherman	Age 20	Popham Beach

The following article is one I took from an old newspaper, September 22, 1883:

"At Popham the workmen are hastening forward the Life Saving Station which will be one of the first in accommodation, equipment and appearance on the coast. It is situated near the bar just south of the billiard saloon, and will contain boathouse, sleeping rooms, kitchen, dining room etc. It will be finished and in working order next month. At Damariscove a similar station is to be located, but this will not be completed before another season."

The station went by the name U.S. Life Saving Station for a number of years, but was later called Hunniwell's Beach Life Saving Station and even later Kennebec River Coast Guard Station.

At the beginning, the station was manned only during the winter months or from September 1 to May 1. The men went back to their own work as fishermen, pilots, etc.

The members of the crew were fellows from Georgetown and Popham, and each was allowed to go home a few hours a week. Lyman Oliver said he usually had time for a bath, change of clothes and a good meal.

One day after the station had been maintained a few years, some of the officials came to put the men through some of their drills and were surprised to find how long it took to put the boat off the beach. The crew explained their trouble was that the tide coming in at a certain

Driftwood from Popham Sands

angle on the beach would take them half way up the beach before they could get through the surf. Not long after that it was decided to find a new location for the station and a new site was acquired in December 1888 up near the steamboat wharf (where it still sits today), but the old site was not abandoned until 1889.

Zina H. Spinney was captain of the station for awhile, also Harvey Berry. It was while he was stationed at Popham that Captain Zina Spinney had a house built (the present house of the late Herbert Sprague). Uncle George Oliver built it from a picture of a house that Captain Spinney saw in a magazine.

In 1924 Christopher Marr, another of the old Hunniwell's Life Saving Station crew, moved into the house of Zina Spinney and later bought it. Mr. Marr in 1926 had served thirty-one years in the Coast Guard, every one which had been at Hunniwell's Beach station. Mr. Marr was in the service when patrolling the beach was one of the duties of the men.

A newspaper item of November 12, 1915, states, "Captain Harvey Berry and crew of the Hunniwell's Beach station were given an opportunity to a distress call from a six ton auxiliary, *Vigilant*, which was in distress 11 miles off Seguin. They were some relieved when the crew reached them."

Coast Guard Lifeboat Stations at Fletcher's Neck, Biddeford Pool and at Popham Beach, at the mouth of the Kennebec River, were closed October 15, 1971. The Coast Guard announced that the closings were an economic measure, but the areas would be covered by planes and boats from bases at Portland, Boothbay Harbor and Portsmouth, N.H. The following announcement ran in the local paper:

> The General Services Administration announces the sale of the Kennebec River Lifeseaboat Station at Popham Beach, Phippsburg, ME to Robert D. Binney of Duxbury,

MA. The property being sold by the Government consists of a wood frame two-story dwelling, a wood frame boathouse and a garage. There is no land included in the sale.

Fort Baldwin

Fort Baldwin, situated on Sabino Hill overlooking Atkins Bay at Popham Beach, was named in honor of Jeduthan Baldwin of Woburn, Massachusetts, an engineer of the Revolutionary War. It is the fourth fort to be built at Popham. The first was Fort St. George built by George Popham's colony in 1607. The second fort was built on the site of the present Fort Popham when the war of Austrian Secession seemed a certainty. The third is the present Fort Popham constructed soon after President Lincoln's election.

The land for Fort Baldwin was purchased by the United States in 1902 and 1904-05 from Nathanial Perkins and Mr. and Mrs. Anson Oliver. It comprised the better part of the top of Sabino Hill. It was originally a part of the Lyman Oliver property, so a deed had to be given by them to cross over their property to get to the Fort Baldwin property. This is the present road in use today. The land at the foot of the hill on the north side of the road where the cars park was also sold along with Mr. Perkin's house.

Before construction could begin on the fort in May of 1905, the ledge at the top and side of the hill had to be blasted in order to set the fort back far enough to be concealed from anything coming into the river and the surrounding countryside. The blasted area was camouflaged later by juniper bushes and small trees.

A long wharf and pier connecting it to the shore property was built by Henry Carlton of Woolwich in 1909. Lighters brought the material to the wharf, and it was taken to the top of the hill by means of flat cars run partly by chains propelled by steam engines.

Driftwood from Popham Sands

Battery at Fort Baldwin.

A trestle that supported the tracks went over the town road, so the people on the point had to go under the trestle to get to the village. The engine house sat on a large flat ledge on the right at the foot of the hill.

Fort Baldwin consists of three batteries: Cogan, Hardman and Hawley. Until some time in the 1940s, a sign at the foot of the right-of-way to the fort gave this information. Alongside the sign was a large flag pole. A number of years ago as I was cleaning up along the side of the road, I found some of the cement blocks that held the guide lines to the pole.

The first battery was named for Lt. Patrick Cogan of the Continental Army, who died August 21, 1778. Two three-inch guns weighing about five ton apiece were mounted there.

The second battery was named after Captain John Hardman, who died as a prisoner of war, September 1, 1780. On this battery

Florence Oliver

Army barracks for Fort Baldwin in World War I, 1918, in the field at the head of the government wharf. Site of archeological dig of Fort George 1990-2010. Photo by Ernest W. Oliver.

Barracks at Fort Baldwin in World War I, by the house, in the field.

Driftwood from Popham Sands

was mounted a disappearing gun of six inches that was raised only to fire and then was lowered so as not to disclose its location. The range was taken at the observatory station located on the battery along side with the electrical equipment. The shaft for this gun is still visible.

The third battery was named for Brevet Major Joseph P. Hawley, U.S. Volunteer, who served during the Civil War and died in 1905. It contained two six-inch pedestal guns each weighing about ten tons. The fort was finished and the last gun mounted by May of 1912.

Fort Baldwin was one of a number of forts constructed under a program for sea coast defense with the idea of protecting Bath and its shipbuilding industry. Fort Baldwin was the only fort built in twentieth-century Maine.

Uncle Lyme was the first Mainer to be hired on the building of the fort and the last to be released. His last job was to help mount the guns. He was later hired to go to Mount Desert Island and help mount those guns as well.

Work progressed slowly. It wasn't until the spring of 1914 that the War Department started on the construction of barracks and an electrical plant, the latter being most essential, for without search lights, the guns would be useless at night. The barracks for the soldiers ran lengthwise from the shore at Atkins Bay to the town road, where the parking lot is today.

During World War I, the 4th Company, Maine Coast Artillery, a National Guard unit from Bath, was assigned to man the two six-inch gun batteries, and regulars from the Coast Artillery were assigned to mine defense, including the three guns at Battery One, which was designed for close defense of the mine field. (The mouth of the Kennebec River was heavily mined to keep ships from entering the river. Boats coming regularly into

Florence Oliver

Tower at Fort Baldwin. Built during World War II. Photo by Mrs. Ernest W. Oliver.

the river were notified as to the location of the mines.)

The source of water for the fort was Silver Lake. Alongside the state road coming into Popham, a pipeline ran from the corner on what is known as Isaacsons and the state property, along the side of the town road to Atkins Bay and the government wharf to the top of the hill to a large storage tank, which was taken down after the war. Men from the National Guard arrived just in time to take to the task with pick and shovel.

There wasn't much to offer the soldiers in the way of social life at Popham except for local dances, entertainment at Society Hall and movies controlled from an electrical plant that sat across the road from the hall. After the arrival of the boys from Bath, the 4th Company Artillery Corps, with the other soldiers stationed there, the soldiers' population far exceeded that of the locals.

A steamer boat ran between Popham Beach and Bath. It carried the mail, passengers and freight, making one trip a day in the winter and two in the summer, making landings at Phippsburg Center, West Georgetown, Parker Head, Cox's Head and Bay Point on signal. The roads were not paved then, and travelling in the winter and spring at times was almost impossible.

From a Bath paper of 1917: "Mess fund for the 1st Company Fort Baldwin will be added to through the fall and winter months by money obtained from rent of the armory. This hall has been thoroughly renovated for dancing purposes. Hiram Stevens' orchestra will play and he has installed a new piano, which will be kept constantly in tune."

Early in September of 1917 the soldiers of the 4th Company were given orders to prepare to go to the Philippine Islands.

In March of 1923, Congress authorized the disposal of certain military reservations no longer needed for military purposes, so under the suggestions of Governor Percival Baxter, Fort Baldwin, including buildings, was purchased by the state of Maine for the price of $5,000, with the stipulation it be used for a state park, reserving to the U.S. government reversion to the title if the property ever was put to any other use. All armaments were removed, and for a while a caretaker was appointed to look after the property but soon was discontinued for lack of funds. Soon the public began to vandalize the place, tearing out wires, breaking glass. During the depression years, all the doors and manhole covers were stolen for scrap.

During World War II, Fort Baldwin and Fort Popham were manned again. This time the guns were mounted on wheels. Barracks were built on the hill as well as a large defense tower, which is still standing.

It was in December 1941 that the soldiers arrived at Fort Baldwin from Fort Preble, Portland Harbor. It was an especially cold winter, the temperature ran below zero for several days at a time, and no preparations had been made for their livelihood. When the first group arrived, they erected a tent in the corner of the marsh where you turn from the state road to go up to Fort Baldwin. We went by one day and they were trying to do some cooking—when they weren't competing with the wind to keep the tent intact. Until barracks could be erected on the hill, the soldiers occupied the library, Society Hall, the former light keepers' dwelling at Fort Popham, the Coast Guard Station and even the batteries at Fort Baldwin. At least they had some heat in these quarters.

The roads were much better than in World War I, and details of men were driven to Bath every day and evening for recreation.

The Lion's Club in Bath was able to get some material from a house that was being torn down to make room for expansion of Bath Iron Works, and they donated it to the soldiers for a recreation hall. One of the soldiers had had some experience in building

Driftwood from Popham Sands

chimneys, so a nice fieldstone fireplace was added. Furnishings were received through a plea in the Bath newspaper, and soon it was well furnished. When the building was finished, they held a dedication service and invited the Lion's Club to participate. It was dedicated "The Lion's Den." After the soldiers left, it was torn down.

We all gained some knowledge of training during the time the soldiers were stationed here. They used the field north of our house for a training and parade ground—and if you have never witnessed the maneuvering on a parade ground, you don't know what you have missed. The soldiers came down every day and practiced with bayonets on an improvised victim of a burlap bag filled with hay tied to a post. I had great sympathy for the enemy. When this group was ordered to overseas duty, Battery One replaced it and was there until the close of the war.

There were some amusing things that happened, and this is one that happened to me. The second detail of men was nearly all southerners, and it was an unusually hot day in August when they arrived at Popham. Truckload after truckload went up on the hill until they couldn't take anymore, so the rest had to wait at the foot of the hill. While they waited, they got out to stretch their legs and look around a bit. Finally they decided to look for some drinking water. Our house being the nearest, they came to the door asking for water, so I gave them some glasses and a pail and pointed to the well curb. Uncle Lyme was watching from the window, and I finally got the idea he was enjoying himself by the sound of his chuckling. I went to the door to see how things were going. They were all standing there looking down into a well of about ten foot of water not knowing a thing to do. After deciding that their arms weren't long enough to reach the water, they turned to look at the house. I immediately pointed to the well pole and instantly knew I had made a mistake, so I went out and showed them how to

Florence Oliver

Lion's Den at Fort Baldwin given in 1944 by the Lion's Club at Bath, Maine, to the soldiers at Fort Baldwin, World War II, for a recreation room. The building was torn down in Bath to make room for the expansion of Bath Iron Works and rebuilt at Popham. It included a large hand-built stone fireplace built by one of the soldiers. It was demolished by the government after the war.

haul up a pail of water. I guess every man got a drink. About an hour later I went to find my pail and found it empty on the door step—but at least it wasn't at the bottom of the well.

One of the exciting things that happened was the firing of the guns for practice. We were notified of the firing so we could open the windows, remove articles that were apt to jar off the shelves, etc. We were behind the guns and under the hill, so it didn't bother us very much, but the houses over in the village and the cottages on the beach were either under the guns or in front of them and some of them received a lot of damage.

A few times there was an alert at night, and the jeeps with the officers came down off the hill followed by trucks of soldiers, and it seemed as though they took the corners on two wheels. It made me kind of nervous. Ernest worked nights at the iron works in Bath, and I was alone with two small children and an old man of eighty-seven years. As soon as it got dark, we had to cover the windows with blackout curtains, which I detested, as well as the gas rationing, which kept so many of the cottage owners from coming to the beach. The soldiers had a few of their own cars parked in the field where the guard could not detect them from the guardhouse, and we often found gas cans around the back of the house where they had brought gas down from off the hill unknown to the officers.

Another amusing thing that happened that following winter was the fact that very few of the soldiers had ever seen snow. We had one bad storm that put everything out of business for a few days. Our road was drifted so bad that the town plow couldn't do a thing with it. They had sent for a rotary plow but before they got there, the soldiers came down off the hill to try and get a jeep through. The snow hadn't drifted so badly on the hill, but when they got to the town road, they were up to their waists rolling around and helping each other up. What a show! One of the soldiers' wives, who rented a cottage off the beaten path, was so scared she went to Bath for the remainder of her stay.

After the War

After the soldiers left it seemed quiet for a while, but as soon as the gas rationing was over and the cottage folks started to return, life went on as before.

Fort Baldwin was very popular for a while after the war with the summer tourists and cottagers. The tower was of equal importance. Finally the barracks and officers quarters were sold and removed, except for the tower. One gets a spectacular view of the river, Atkins Bay, Bay Point, Cox's Head, the islands, a peek of the ocean and a view of the countryside for miles.

Florence Oliver

One day, sometime after the soldiers left, I heard a knock at the door. When I opened it, there stood a man who identified himself as an FBI agent. He handed me a package of paper matches that had the name of Oliver written on them. I told him that neither of us smoked and that the only time Ernest had been up there was when he went on business and had gone up in company with an officer. While we were talking, the sheriff appeared around from the front of the house where my four-year-old daughter was playing. The fort up to this time was off limits to the public, but I knew my daughter had seen some of the neighbors and cottage people go up there. All I could think of was the old saying "Out of the mouths of babes." As soon as I could after the men left, I went to hunt her up and asked her what the nice man had said to her.

She said, "He asked me if anybody went up on the hill?"

I said, "What did you tell him?"

"I said everybody."

"Did he ask you anything else?"

"He asked me when they went up."

I presumed he meant evenings or weekends when the people were more or less apt to be around, so I asked her, "What did you tell him?"

She said "I told him that sometimes they went up on Mondays and sometimes they went up on Fridays, was that all right?"

I said "I think that was fine," and got out of the way before she heard me laugh.

Today Fort Baldwin comes under the head of the Popham Beach State Park and rangers check it and maintain a parking lot in the field by the shore. Nobody knows what the future holds in store for it.

Over the years many of the soldiers have been back to visit the forts and the few people remain who were there at the time. Most of

Driftwood from Popham Sands

them remark on the changes, especially the steamboats, Society Hall, the Coast Guard Station and some of the old stores. World War II soldiers didn't see so many changes but, of course, there were some.

∽

I wrote a letter to the editor of the *Coastal Journal*:

"In regards to the picture in the *Coastal Journal* of June 6, this is a scene of the village at Popham Beach with Bay Point, Kennebec Point, Stage and Salters Islands and one of the Sugar Loaf [peaks] in the background, taken about 1910.

At the extreme left of the picture stands the government flag pole at the gate to Fort Popham, where the Sergeants resided. The next building is the Haley and Marr store, which also housed the post office with Mr. Ephraim Marr as postmaster. The next large building at the end of the dock that led to the landing where the steamboat *Virginia* docked was the old John H. Stacey store. The house, across the road, partly hidden by the store, was the home of Charles C. Haley, part owner of the Haley and Marr store. This house was moved soon after this picture was taken to near the Coast Guard Station at the end of the old steamboat wharf and is now owned by Mrs. Geneva Moody.

The large two-story house with the cupola on the roof was the home of John H. Stacey, who conducted a rooming house. It is now the guest house of Fred. H. Spinney. The small house, at the right in the foreground, was the home of John Haley, who was a member of the Hunniwell's Beach Life Saving Station. The large building at the right of John H. Stacey's in the background was the Riverside Hotel, which was taken down, and later a store was erected by Mr. and Mrs. Laurence Taylor. This hotel was very popular

Florence Oliver

and folks came back every summer for a number of years.

The low white house in the center of the picture was the home of Uncle Nat Perkins, as he was called, later the home of Mrs. Marguerite McNulty, and the large stable belonged to the Riverside Hotel.

The large houseboat and stable was owned by Haley and Marr and used in the buying of fish.

The house in the front of the chapel belonged to Mr. Marr, and the one to the left of the chapel belonged to Mr. Hiram Stevens, grandfather of Bob Stevens, who runs the Sea Acre Camps. The house to the right of Mr. Marr's was a boarding house run by Mr. Calvin Oliver, later known as Mr. Stanley Hyde's.

Mr. Frank Moore lived in the houseboat at the extreme right of the picture.

This picture brings back childhood memories, as I have always made my home here. This particular view I see every time I leave my house to go over into the village. I have seen many changes over the years."

The *Coastal Journal* didn't see fit to use this letter or even acknowledge it for some reason. Helen, our postal carrier, got the five dollars, and another letter was pointed out by someone who told of more than the picture of what she remembered about Popham. It was too bad as so many people looked forward to reading Ernest's letter when they found he had written in.

Old Trading Post

During the War of 1812, a man named Joshua Shaw carried on a trading post at Popham on the government reservation, where Fort Popham stands today, and called it "Shaw's Trading Post." History tells us that the original post burned and "The Yellow House" that replaced it was built on or near the old site. It was razed in 1908 to make room for a dwelling house for the keeping of a light along side of Fort Popham. Some have been known to confuse this with "The Tavern" which stood nearly half way on the ridge between the fort and the old entrance to the fort property.

Shaw lived in a large house of seventeen rooms, which he built in 1793, known as "The Shaw Mansion" next to what is known today as Silver Lake. It was razed about 1891, the oldest house at that time on Popham, to make room for the "Stone House" that stands there today (Isaacsons). Shaw's house sat nearer to the road than the present one and in the 1850s was known as the "Irving House." Uncle George and Uncle Lyme's mother was from the Irving family.

When they were excavating for the foundation of the stone house for Mr. Ingraham, Uncle Lyme said that shells, driftwood and even an old fireplace were unearthed. He said it looked as though the sea might have come back as far as there at some time, making Silver Lake a salt water pond. Even in later years, in the spring when the pond was high, the water would seek its way out into the bogs back of the cottages, and today, at the highest tides, it is almost back to those same bogs.

The Native Americans would come over to the Kennebec from Harpswell by way of an old Native American trail. When they left the Trading Post, they would go out of the village as far as the Irving Pond, now Silver Lake, and then turn sharp right in a westerly direction up over the ledges and swing along the side of Atkins Bay to the big marsh. Later the trail was widened by wheel tracks and used in the spring, as the road from the pond to the marsh was deep sand and it was impossible to drive a horse faster than walk over it. In the spring it was unsafe on account of frost holes.

Florence Oliver

At the March town meeting in 1860, it was voted to accept a road from the Irving Pond to the government property line near Fort Popham. This was the beginning of a town road at Popham. At one time one had to go over several sand bars to go from Lyman Oliver's house to the village.

On a deed from the Olivers to James Jones is the following, "Except and reserving to the owners of the Lyman Oliver farm and their heirs and assigns a wagon road through this property unobstructed by gates, bars, fences or any other obstruction that might be placed upon."

Years back as they were laying out a road across the big marsh, their intentions were to go to the right of the little island in the marsh going out to Popham. The idea was to make a shorter route. In the process of sounding, they discovered an old corduroy road and the logs were in such good condition, they decided to continue along the old way. For those who might not know, a corduroy road is one where the logs are laid crosswise through a swampy place.

Owen's *History of Bath* speaks of a settlement made at Small Point in 1718. A road was laid out from Small Point to the Sagadahoc River (Kennebec), so it could have been a part of this road.

In August 1716, the Proprietors in Boston voted to send our sloop, the *Pejepscot,* with 4,000 foot of boards to Small Point and start building a fishing town. In September Captain Peter Newell was instructed to have a cart path cut from Small Point Harbor to the Sagadahoc (Kennebec) River adjacent to Arrowsic in the most convenient way the land will allow. Remains of log work on this first road were still visible early in the twentieth century.

Driftwood from Popham Sands

The Popham Dig

Phippsburg, Maine
June 16, 1962

I, Ernest W. Oliver, hereby, grant the State of Maine permission to carry on archaeological exploration on my property under the direction of Wendell S. Hadlock.

All historical and other material culture found on my property is to be returned to me, the owner, after it has been used for study purposes.

I reserve the right to terminate this agreement at any time.

It is further agreed that the State of Maine will replace all dirt and objects removed.

>Ernest W. Oliver
>Alice R. Erskine
>(Signed) Witness
>David W. Eaton
>(Signed) Witness

When talk about a "dig" at Popham first took place, some of the state park commissioners came down and met with Ernest Oliver, the park ranger at the time, at the site of the George Popham Memorial.

On learning that the state did not own any land in that immediate area, they decided any digging that was done would be done on land owned by the state across the road at the head of the old government wharf.

Afterwards they got Ernest's permission to dig across the head of our field along the edge of the bank, and across the north end

Florence Oliver

Governor Reed at "The Dig" at Popham. Fort Popham in background. 1965.

"The Dig" at Popham Beach 1964-1965 on Ernest Oliver's property.

of the field alongside of our house. They said they were looking for foundations.

Ernest was always sorry that they didn't dig deeper, for clam shells could be seen in the bank from the shore about three feet from the top of the ground, and without a doubt this had to have been the top of the ground at one time.

They also dug on state property up around the bay. We had hoped they would dig on the extreme end of the point where years ago, according to the "Ancient Dominion of Maine" a large impression dug into the bank resembled that of a ship. When Lyman Oliver bought the land it was still prominent in practically the only place a ship could have been launched on that point. Maybe some old tools or pieces of material might have been found.

The site of the Popham Colony was definitely established at the mouth of the Kennebec in 1964-65. Archaeological finds pinpointed the actual site on Sabino Head. A marker has been placed on the site.

The discoveries included a bale seal. It is made of lead about the size of a quarter, which merchants in the seventeenth century attached to bolts of cloth to prove that they contained twenty yards of material; the seal from the end of a latten spoon, a brass-like alloy in use in England at the time of the founding of the colony.

The 1964-1965 excavation was not the first dig at Popham. In the newspaper files dated August 4, 1883: "At Popham last week a party of diggers unearthed arrow heads and pottery. One of the pitchers dug from the sand by an enterprising youth from Massachusetts was the recipient of a five dollar bill as soon as it was unearthed."

From some of Uncle Nat Perkins' notes, he tells that the land in back of his house and the chapel was a Native American campground. As a boy he had picked up handfuls of Native American

Florence Oliver

wampum, which looked like bits of clay pipe (beads), and arrow heads (flint) eight and ten inches long.

We have a few arrow heads that were plowed out from the land in front of our house at Popham.

Uncle Lyme Oliver used to tell about some Native Americans who used to visit at Malcolm's Cove (across Atkins Bay) every year for some kind of memorial. One old Native American used to come and visit with Uncle Lyme and Uncle George Oliver. They would dig clams and have a big campfire but their visit was short.

Chapter Three

Boats

Since the beginning of Popham Beach in 1607, boats have played an important part on the Kennebec.

In a letter to the editor of the Richmond, Virginia, *Times Dispatch* published August 3, 1957, D.G. Maclaren Boyden, historiographer of the Episcopal Diocese of Virginia, wrote an interesting comparison of current celebrations of the 350th anniversary of Jamestown and Popham settlements. In his comparison of the two celebrations, Dr. Boyden wrote in part as follows: "The Popham celebration is based upon the indefinable fact that in the life of the Popham settlement 1607-1608, the settlers built the first seagoing vessel, which continued in existence and in active service between England and Jamestown for perhaps twenty years after the town of its builders had been abandoned. According to one report, it was eventually wrecked on the Irish coast while bearing a cargo of tobacco to England."

Sailing was the major means of transportation, although steamboats were used on the river as early as the 1800s. The following is a quote from the *Bath Independent*, June 6, 1896: "Under Folks Views" by John Marr calling it "The Devil." When our downriver ancestors saw the first steamer approaching, to steam up to Bath, seventy years ago, the alarm felt by fishermen is described by one who first saw *The Maine.*

The first steamer on the Kennebec was the *Tom Thumb* as early as 1818. She was an open boat propelled by side wheels. A century later the river claimed to have the most complete steamboat service on the East coast.

In 1823, the Kennebec and Boston Steamboat Line became the first permanent coastwise steamboat line north of Cape Cod. Popham was the only local landing made by the Boston steamers on the Maine coast over the years on this line.

Sailboats continued to be popular. On the walls of the old David T. Percy cottage, now Robert Stevens', in September 1881, he had recorded that from the piazza looking seaward, he had counted 95 vessels, most of them sailing from or going in the Kennebec. August 1885, he recorded 120 vessels in the bay; and August 15, 1896, he counted and put down 96 vessels observed. From the *Bath Independent* August 1897: "Saturday many summer visitors at Popham and vicinity enjoyed a rare sight, the privilege of seeing 47 sails assembled on Parker's Flats. Most of them sailed up the Kennebec without assistance from tugs." Tugs were in great demand on the river. One local tug was named Popham for the chief of the first colony. Other local ones were the *Union, Echo* and *Robson.*

Steamboats probably influenced the most growth of Popham Beach. The little steamer *Creedmore* was supposedly the first to run on the regular route from *Popham* to Bath. She was a small boat but much in demand as the only means of transportation to the mouth of the river. Steamboats brought a lot of business to Popham by way of vacationers, excursions, freight and so forth.

In 1881 at a meeting of the board of directors of the Popham Beach Company, Messrs. Perkins and Stacey were appointed agents of the company. It was decided to build a wharf on the east shore with a pier and later a pavilion. The wharf was completed in 1882.

Driftwood from Popham Sands

Left: Sabino, *a steam-powered boat ran the Kennebec River helmed by Captain Jim Perkins. The Sabino is now in Mystic, Connecticut at the Mystic Seaport museum.*

Below: Sabino *in Mystic Seaport, CT, with Edith Oliver and Margaret Oliver Ladue.*

Certificate of Stock in Popham Beach Wharf Company, issued July 16, 1913 for one share of capital stock, value $10, issued to George A. Oliver.

Copy of Popham Beach Steamboat Company receipt for freight charges totaling $.65, July 17, 1924.

"Popham Day 1921" ticket.

"Steamer 'Percy V' Round Trip."

Driftwood from Popham Sands

The Popham Beach Steamboat Company was formed in 1904 and continued until 1927. It built a wharf jutting out into Atkins Bay. This was used by the smaller steamers. We have a certificate for one share at ten dollars for the Popham Beach Wharf Company dated 1913 and signed by J.H. Stacey as treasurer. This may have been about the time they extended the wharf out to the edge of the bay opposite the fort. At the end of the pier was the "Dog Hole," a place dug out where they could moor the boats at night. Prior to this they had to take them to the Eastern Steamship wharf.

The *Ransom B. Fuller*, one of the most popular in her day, was built in Bath in 1902 by the New England Shipbuilding Company of Bath. She was the first steamboat launched after the Kennebec line was taken over by the Eastern Steamship Company.

One of the steamboats that I remember was the *City of Rockland*. She went into commission on the Kennebec line of the Eastern Steamship Company in 1914. She went aground on Dix's Island in the Kennebec in 1924. She ran on the line with the steamship *City of Bangor*, another one I remember.

These steamers made a run to Gardiner or Hallowell. They would arrive in Bath early in the morning and take on freight and passengers for the morning run up river, stopping at frequent landings on the way, returning early in the evening.

She would stop at Popham and then on to Boston. The two ships would pass somewhere at sea. I do not think they made a daily trip up river, possibly once or twice a week.

In 1901 we find another *Virginia* at the mouth of the Kennebec. Although she was not built at Popham, she was built for the Bath/Popham run and was designed by J. Arthur Stevens of Popham Beach. She was built at the New England shipyard in Bath and continued on that route until 1922. Later on she ran on the Boothbay run, making trips to Gardiner and Hallowell, where I remember her.

Florence Oliver

While she was on the Popham run, she ran under Captain James E. Perkins. Eddie McNulty served as purser on the Popham line for twenty-seven years. Ernest Oliver started on his steamboat career under Captain Jim soon after the *Virginia* started on that run. He served in every capacity while he was on her, the *Sabino* and the *Isleford*, often taking the boat in the absence of Captain Jim. When his license came up for renewal during World War II, he couldn't leave his job in the Bath Iron Works to go to Portland to take the test, and that ended his boating career.

The first thing he remembered doing when he went to work on the boats was to learn to splice a piece of rope and to clean brass. That was one of Captain Jim's strong points. He also served under Captain Frank S. Oliver and Fred Hodgekins.

From the **Bath Independent**: March 1916

The new spare boat of the Popham Beach Steamboat Company arrived at Popham Friday afternoon, March 20, 1916, from Portland, making the trip across the bay at 28 miles in three hours and ten minutes. The boat was piloted by Captain Llewellyn Oliver of Popham, a machinist from Portland looking after the engine. The new boat is the *Two Brothers*, a gasoline yacht capable of carrying one hundred passengers and of making nine or ten knots. Her name is to be changed when she is put into commission on the Popham line.

In May the *Two Brothers* was renamed the *George Popham* in honor of the first Chief of the Popham Colony.

From the Bath Independent June 1916

The first excursion party on the Kennebec this summer in the *George Popham* was that brought up Friday evening by Captain L.J. Oliver from Popham, there being thirty natives and summer visitors, chiefly young people who at-

Driftwood from Popham Sands

Florence Oliver

Clockwise from upper left: Sunbeam *was a Seacoast Mission boat that traveled along the coast to minister to residents on the islands, Coast Guard Stations and other remote populations;* Steamboat Landing, Popham Beach. S.S. Ransom B. Fuller *leaving Popham Beach wharf;* Scow carrying a car across Atkins Bay to Popham Beach from Bay Point during mud season *and* The George Popham, *run between Bath and Popham as a freight boat as late as 1934-1935.*

tended the movies here and met after the last show, leaving at eleven P.M.

After the *Sabino* left the Popham route, I believe the *George Popham* was the regular mail boat for a number of years. I think that Captain Oliver bought the boat and bid on the mail contract. I can remember going to Cox's Head and Popham several times on her. Ernest Oliver ran the engine for a while, also Merton Oliver, and I think Leslie Dyer was on her when she was sold. That was the last of the mail coming by water.

Another boat that played an important part for a while in the lives of those living at Popham was the *Sunbeam*, a vessel owned by the Maine Seacoast Mission, which visited and ministered to families on the islands and lonely headlands of Maine from Kittery to Calais. Within the far-flung parish of the Sea Coast Mission in 1940 were fifty-two lighthouses and twelve Coast Guard Stations, many of which were visited during the winter and at Christmas time with gifts of candy, toys, knitted articles, etc., for the children and elderly folk.

The first vessel built in 1905 was the Friendship sloop *Hope;* the second a power boat called the *Morning Star.* The name *Sunbeam* was given to the third, a gift of John S. Kennedy (a resident of Mount Desert), the name having been suggested by the small daughter of a lighthouse keeper. It might interest the reader to know that the small daughter was none other than Mrs. Mildred Sprague of Popham Beach, whose favorite hymn was "Jesus Wants Me For A Sunbeam." There have been several Sunbeams to date. *Sunbeam III* was sold to Research Charters, Inc. of Camden for charter to universities and groups engaged in oceanographic studies. *Sunbeam IV* in 1965 was sixty-five feet long, all metal and diesel-powered, the sixth in line of the Maine Sea Coast Mission

Society to serve island people along the coast of Maine.

In 1940 an author by the name of Edwin Valentine Mitchell took the cruise around the islands with the Reverend Neil Bousefield, superintendent of the mission. Later he wrote a book and named it *Anchors to Windward*, based on the life of the islanders, storms, shipwrecks and quaint island characters. Popham was the next to the last stop, Seguin being the last. He came to our house and visited with Uncle George and Lyme Oliver and he mentions this visit in his book, which we are fortunate to own. Unfortunately, the trip to Seguin never materialized, due to the heavy surf that made landing impossible.

A few years after that we had a regular minister in town so they only stopped at the Coast Guard Station, but the gifts were still sent for a number of years.

The Joseph Luther

Among the many wrecks at the mouth of the Kennebec River was the wreck of the *Joseph Luther*, a New London three-masted schooner that went ashore January 1901 on the ledge northeast of Pond Island known as Whaleback Rock. She had discharged a cargo of iron at one of the Sewall shipyards in Bath and was being towed by the tug *Knickerbocker* to Clark's Cove for a load of ice. When abreast the Lower Sugar Loaf Island, the hawser connecting the tug and the schooner parted. With a strong south wind blowing, the ship was helpless.

Captain Zina Spinney and his crew from the Kennebec River Life Saving Station put off in a surf boat and, with the help of a Lyle gun, succeeded in shooting a line to the stranded craft. One by one the captain and a crew of six men were saved, also the tiger cat, which later became the station's mascot.

Driftwood from Popham Sands

The vessel was built in New London, Connecticut, in 1891 and was owned by Charles Berry of New London.

The remains of the wreck were salvaged by Captain Anson Oliver, a river pilot with a volunteer crew of the locals. Uncle Lyme Oliver was one of the crew, and we have a large platter as a souvenir of the wreck. Uncle Lyme said every time he turned around on the stricken vessel, the platter landed between his feet and he had to take it ashore to get rid of it. It is a large white platter with rounded corners decorated with a pale blue trim. An English mark is on the back. Every year on Thanksgiving, as the platter bears the turkey to the table, we always speak of the *Joseph Luther*.

Chapter Four

Society Hall

Probably by the time Society Hall was torn down, it could have told as good a story about Popham Beach as ever has been written. For years most community activity circled around that spot—dances, entertainments, suppers, meetings and even religious services.

In 1887, the Ladies Sewing Circle saw the need, until the chapel was built, for a building in the community for such things, and a committee was picked to see what could be done about some land. Mr. and Mrs. P. O. Vickery of Augusta finally came to their aid and deeded to the Circle the piece of land 50 by 70 feet where today sits the garage of Barbara Bentley on the north side of the road as you swing to go towards Fort Popham and Spinney's restaurant. Uncle George Oliver was a member of the board of trustees for years; in fact he was the only member left at the time of his death in 1942.

The following is the list of the women who belonged to the Ladies Sewing Circle:

"That I, Peleg O. Vickery of Augusta, State of Maine in consideration of one dollar paid by: Frances Haley (Mrs. James), Emma Perkins (Mrs. James), Sarah A. Clark (Mrs. Henry M.), Alma E. Perkins (Mrs. Nathaniel), J. M. Oliver (Mrs. Elbridge), Fannie Oliver (Mrs. Calvin), Emma Oliver (Mrs. George A.), Maria Haley

(Mrs. John), Almira Marr (Mrs. Ephraim), Eva Stacey (Mrs. John H.). December 29, 1887 Before me John Stacey, Justice of Peace..."

Everyone helped in her own way to pay for the hall, and many a supper was served by the womenfolk, followed by a dance. That was the time of square dances. Gus Small used to call and Frank Oliver did for many years. When I asked Uncle Lyme Oliver if he ever danced, he told me he did some, but one leg never seemed to cooperate with the other. I think he used to dance the square dances, but it was the round dances he never mastered.

During the winter months when there were not too many to attend a dance, they would call over to Small Point, Parker's Head, Bay Point. Hiram Stevens would come down in the boat at night to play the fiddle. Mrs. Millie Spinney from Bay Point would come over to play the piano, and they were all set for a dance.

One year about 1910 a guest at the Riverside Hotel noticed that several of the young people weren't dancing. He got permission from the trustees and started dancing lessons. He had quite a few pupils, Ernest Oliver being one of them. After a few lessons he would invite some of the older ones to come in and dance with his pupils for practice. They learned the waltz and two step by the end of the first season.

When the hall was fairly new, they put on a few plays directed by Gus Huse of Bath. One of the plays was "Ten Nights in a Barroom." Uncle Lyme played the part of the barkeeper. In the play a little girl coming into the barroom to get her father, who was a frequent visitor there, gets hit in the head with a glass. An old Irish lady who lived around there didn't understand it was just a play and held it against Mr. Oliver, for a long time.

Later years, Ed McNulty used to run the dances. They would have ice cream that came down on the boat on the afternoon trip. In those days the ice cream came in what they

Florence Oliver

At left, Society Hall, Popham Beach. It burned to the ground in the late 1940s. From a postcard by Otis N.E. Card.

called bricks. They used to cut about six slices out of a brick. Often times they either over ordered or the crowd was smaller than usual and there would be a lot left over, so Ed would call all the kids around and peddle it out to them. Not bothering to dirty any dishes, he would lay a slice in their hand. Many kids were seen running to the door, lapping ice cream from their hands and wrists.

One could go on and on about the events that went on in the old hall, but it all came to end like all the old halls of that time. If we could have collected the money due us for the damage from the firing of the guns at Fort Baldwin during World War II and the use of it for the soldiers, we could have made the necessary repairs and kept it, but there were a few that didn't want it due to the noise and parking problems, and the expense was too much with the chapel repairs, so it was torn down.

This left the neighborhood with no place to conduct any social activities until the Popham Circle came up with the idea to ask the town for the use of the schoolhouse until they decided what they were going to do with it. The chairs, dishes, etc., salvaged from the hall were taken up there, and many a dollar besides good times were benefitted from it. It was later sold to Norman Markham for a shop and afterwards sold for a cottage.

The Popham Chapel

During the 1892 session of Edgecomb's quarterly meeting held with the Boothbay Free Will Baptist Church, it voted to raise a council consisting of the following persons: the Reverend James Boyd of Georgetown, Joseph Nickerson of Edgecomb, G.M. Bowie of Parker's Head and Layman R.F. Hinckley of Georgetown, Deacon F.D. Wyman of Parker's Head, L.S. of Small Point, and James Hunniwell of Woolwich, subject to the call of the Reverend A.C. Brown, having this mission in charge to consider the advisability of organizing a church at Popham Beach in the town of Phippsburg.

The council met at Society Hall at Popham, where religious activities were held July 6, 1892, at 2:30 P.M., and after a discussion, it was voted unanimously to organize a church at a meeting held the same evening of July 6. The following received the right hand of fellowship, which was appropriately administered by the Reverend James Boyd of Georgetown: the Reverend A.C. Brown, Emma Brown, Annie Bowie, Zina H. Spinney, Rachel Spinney, Vesta Jones, Augustus Perkins, and John H. Stacey, all having letters from other churches except sister Annie Bowie and brother Augustus A. Perkins. Other members were taken in but nothing was said about building a church. It is unclear if they thought they were too small a group to take on such a project or whether there

Florence Oliver

was some dissension among the church and the rest of the community. It was not until after a parish was organized in November 9, 1893, that there was any mention of a chapel. At the close of the prayer meeting on Wednesday, December 20, 1893, it was voted to pay over to the treasurer of the parish whatever money there was in the treasury donated towards a chapel, due notice having previously been given.

On November 1, 1893, the inhabitants of Popham Beach were notified and warned to give notice to all interested in organizing a parish to meet in some suitable place. It was signed by John H. Stacey, Notary Public. On November 9, 1893, a meeting was held at Society Hall at 2:30 P.M. and the following officers were elected: the Reverend Joseph Noble, Chairman, John H. Stacey, Clerk, Deacon Zina H. Spinney, Collector and Mrs. Sybil Perkins, Treasurer. After carefully and prayerfully considering the organizing of a parish, it was unanimously voted. The following committees were voted: Building Committee, E.S. Marr, Lyman I. Oliver and John H. Stacey. The committee for locating a site for the chapel was: Frances Haley, Vesta Jones and Eva Stacey. The building committee was instructed to raise donations of money or lands for the purpose of building a chapel to be dedicated wholly for religious purposes and the worship of God.

It was voted to choose five trustees to whom all lands would be conveyed in trust for the parish. The following persons were chosen: Nancy J. Clark, Frances Haley, Alma E. Perkins, Lyman I. Oliver and John H. Stacey. It was voted that the organization be known as the Popham Beach Parish. Mr. Lyman Oliver remained a member of the board of trustees all during the remainder of his ninety-six years.

At a meeting of said parish on November 14, 1893, the building committee reported the location of a lot for the chapel on the south side of the town road just east of E.S. Marr's house. It was unanimously approved and the building committee was given orders to order the frame and boards at once, not to exceed $200. It was voted to add the names of George Oliver and A.M. Hodgkins to the building committee. Deeds of the chapel site were read from the Popham Beach Real Estate and Hotel Association and adopted.

Work continued on the building, weather permitting, but the raising did not take place until May 30, 1894. It was followed by a supper at Society Hall.

Mrs. William Spinney, known to everybody as "Aunt Carrie" drove the first spike in the building of the chapel. Her energy didn't stop there. She was an excellent cook and there never was a supper held at Society Hall that didn't consist of her baking powder biscuits and baked beans.

On April 20, 1894, it was voted to send E.S. Marr to Norway, Maine, to look for windows and, if they were in good condition, to purchase eight circle tops and one circle window, the price not to exceed thirty dollars for the nine windows.

During the summer money came in slowly but faithfully from many interested donors. Labor was scarce as this was the season when most of the locals earned their livelihood.

It was during one of these lulls that the ladies of the village decided to take things in their own hands to get things moving again. They arrived at the chapel and proceeded with saws and hammers right out where all the passers-by could see them. It happened that Uncle George Oliver had charge of that particular project, and he was not too pleased to see women "ruining" what had already been done, so he immediately got a crew together and the womenfolk went back to their housekeeping.

At a meeting in July it was voted to proceed to finish the chapel at once, even if they had to borrow the money. The purchase of the

Florence Oliver

pews was left to the committee, J.H. Stacey and Lyman I. Oliver. Most of the furnishings were bought through the D.T. Percy store at Bath. The committee reported that they could buy 22 pews delivered from Boston for $255, and a pulpit set for $68.50. They were instructed to buy them and voted the committee to see about the carpeting. A donation from the Rockledge guests and others amounted to $75.

One of the money-raising events was a Lawn Party, which was very popular in those days. It was held on the lawn of Frank and Effie Oliver next to the old school house. A guest at the Riverside Hotel erected a small tent on the lawn where she told fortunes, which delighted the guests. Homemade candy and lemonade, also other goodies, were on sale and chances on various things brought in many a dollar. One of the items was a huge fruit cake, which was won by Llewellyn Oliver. Games and music was enjoyed, and everyone helped to make it a success.

Another event was what they called a costume dance. Today it would be called a masquerade. There were costumes of all descriptions, some hired and some original. A lot of effort was put into it for everyone knew it was for a good cause and were glad to contribute to it.

A young lady who used to come to the Riverside in company with whom we later knew as Elsa Kimmouth won a prize as the most original in a pirate's suit.

By November of 1895 the new windows had been installed, making the outside appearance very attractive.

Somewhere over the years, these windows have been made memorial windows by some of their families, having the initials of those in memory.

I do not know all of them but those I recollect are: on the front, right facing the chapel is Irwin M. McIntire; left front,

Driftwood from Popham Sands

Lucy A. Payne, given by Thomas Payne in memory (broken and replaced); east side, blue: John H. Stacey; green: Ephraim S. Marr (broken and replaced); orange: George H. Clark; west side, blue: Sarah Ann Cutting, given in memory by Miss Emma Cutting of Sarah Ann, Ann of Henry and Sarah Cutting (replaced); green: Captain Zina H. Spinney; orange: George E. Macomber. The window inside of the chapel over the door (WCTU), is the Women's Christian Temperance Union and J.M. Perkins, a small one on the front.

We were not able to get the same kind of glass when the windows were replaced, and it seemed more practical to get them replaced to keep out the weather.

The work on the inside now was to get ready for the plasterers. The young boys of the village had picked up wood along the beach all summer to use for this purpose. Every pair of hands was put to use to make the project a success, and not an idea was turned down that would make a few cents for the cause. Sometime in December 1895 they got to work, Uncle Nat Perkins being the head mason. It took many days and nights to get the plaster dried properly. Again the ladies did their bit by taking in lunches to those who sat up at night to keep the fires going.

Judge Hardie, a frequent visitor at the beach, donated the bell for the chapel. It was one of an unusually clear tone, and the people on the south beach had no trouble in hearing it.

The chandelier was purchased through the D.T. Percy store at Bath and creates a lot of interest to anyone entering the chapel. A number of years ago when the chapel underwent a series of repairs, the chandelier was electrified, which enhanced the chapel's stained glass windows when the chandelier was lit.

At last it was done and the date set for the dedication, but a

Florence Oliver

heavy storm turned up and it seemed advisable to postpone it to the next day, October 1, 1896. The following is the program given at that time:

Afternoon
    2:00   Song: "Rock of Ages" Praise Service
    2:30   Sermon by Reverend W.A. Atchly
            Song: "Holy is the Lord"
    3:00   Talks
            M.K. Murray, for Y.M.C.A
            N.G. Jackson, for Y.P.S.C.E
            Kate Spinney, for W.C.T.U.
            "Song of the Soldier"
    3:30   Sermon by Professor J.A. Howe
            Doxology
Evening
    7:00   Prayer, Praise and Social Service
            Song: "Calvary" by Miss Pearl Stacey
    7:45   Sermon, Gilbert L. Harney
    Song: "Son of God"
    8:00   Dedicatory Prayer, Reverend A.F. Dunnels
    Song: "Coronation"

There have been several weddings in the chapel over the years. The first couple to be married was Mr. And Mrs. Alfred E. Rowe in 1897. On their sixtieth anniversary they returned on September 22, 1957, and attended the evening service. Afterwards pictures were taken of the congregation with Mr. And Mrs. Rowe, and then we were all invited over to Spinney's for ice cream. The second couple to be married at the chapel was Pearl Stacey and Dr. Adelbert Williams.

Soon after the turn of the century, the Free Will Baptist Church began to grow smaller as people were leaving and taking their letters of membership to other churches. Soon little interest was shown in those who were left and the parish and trustees took over full responsibility.

Visiting ministers kept the chapel pulpit filled during the summer months. The furnace finally rusted and couldn't be used. Several times subscriptions were taken up for repairs.

After the death of Mr. Ephraim Marr, Lyman I. Oliver found himself sole trustee of the chapel. He consulted a lawyer as to what should be done. On his advice he elected two trustees, his son, Ernest, and Marguerite McNulty, postmistress at that time, to replace the original trustees.

Sometime in the late thirties a bad storm blew off the front of the vestibule of the chapel and caused other damages. New steps were needed, glass replaced, etc. A request to the Davenport Fund in Bath, which would help churches if the request was urgent, brought $200.

By this time we were into World War II, and every man was working at some job, many of them nights, so the work of the chapel just didn't get done.

Finally a welfare worker was hired by the Christian Service Committee of the town to conduct church services, Sunday Schools, etc. During this time, the people were anxious to get the chapel open, but nobody came forward to help on the repairs. Mr. Lyman Oliver refused to let the building be used under the circumstances for fear of somebody getting hurt. Against Mr. Oliver's judgment, a few people got together and made a few repairs and held a service. At the end of the service a meeting was held to form a new parish.

Ernest Oliver and Marguerite McNulty were replaced as trustees, but Mr. Lyman Oliver was kept on as honorary member. After a few years Ernest was again voted in as a trustee, a position he held until his death in 1974.

Florence Oliver

Popham Sewing Circle: Front Row: (L-R) Nancy Spinney, Amy Sprague, Back Row (L-R) Florence Oliver, Geneva Moody, Doris Gilmore, Myra Scott, Olive Crowley.

Soon after this, the Christian Service Committee decided to hire a minister to replace the welfare worker. The chapel was repaired by the help of the Popham Circle, the Davenport Fund and donations from the cottage people. It has been kept in good repair ever since. After the Christian Service Committee disbanded, a group of laymen from the Bath area kept the chapel open in the summer season for as long as I lived at Popham.

The Popham Circle

On May 16, 1941, Frances Robie (now Mrs. John Morse), a social worker in Phippsburg, organized a circle of women at Popham Beach for the purpose of raising money to repair the chapel.

The first meetings were held in the library, and at the second meeting the group decided on the name "Popham Circle."

In the fall of 1946, as the building was not in use, the circle asked permission of the Phippsburg School Committee for the use of the schoolhouse at Popham until the committee had other plans for it. The next few years various projects were carried on there, such as suppers, fairs, and even church services.

Outside of the contributions to the repairs of the chapel, the circle carried on the duties of the parish by remembering the ill and shut-ins with cards and plants, especially at Easter.

Extensive repairs were made to the chapel over the years by the circle, and donations were made from the Davenport Fund, the cottage owners and friends of the chapel. The walls were paneled, ceiling renewed, windows replaced, electricity installed, furnace installed, carpet laid on the pulpit, linoleum installed on the main floor and the pews refinished. The building has had several paint jobs, roof reshingling, new steeple, new steps and a new front door installed from money willed to the circle by Earland Oliver in memory of his father, George Oliver.

From the results of a supper put on jointly by the circle and the Library Association, shrubbery was bought and set out in front of both buildings and a new lawn was made in front of the chapel.

The circle did more for the village than keep the chapel in repair. It was the background for all the social life for the folks who lived there. Birthdays were observed, also Halloween and Christmas. Christmas was always special, with the schoolhouse gaily decorated with evergreen boughs and alder berries, candles and a tree with lights and decorations. The singing of carols and games were enjoyed, and the exchange of gifts and refreshments made a happy evening.

A couple of the most amusing events that took place at the schoolhouse come to mind. At the celebration of a twenty-fifth wedding anniversary of one of the neighbors, we put on a mock

Florence Oliver

wedding. The costumes were donated and borrowed from folks' attics which contributed to the hilarious affair. Fred Spinney was the bride and Ernest Oliver the groom.

Another affair was a fashion show using antique clothes, which was more than popular with the cottage people who saw it. Bathing suits dating back to the first of the century, high buttoned shoes, hoop skirts, a bride's outfit, night gowns and caps, and not forgetting the lingerie, that more than delighted the audience.

These affairs all brought a lot of enjoyment to the residents of Popham, as well as others, even though it entailed a lot of work. We were quite a distance from the nearest community, and traveling conditions weren't always the best.

Slowly the population grew smaller, and today there are a very few year round residents. I understand the circle is still active and carries on the repairs to the chapel.

"Popham Circle Celebrates 25th Anniversary" *Observer*, May 24, 1966, by Florence R. Oliver

On Tuesday, May 22 (1966), members of Popham Circle invited village friends and members of the Extension Service, Fire Auxiliary and Unity Circle to join with them in the celebration of their 25th anniversary.

It was twenty-five years ago on May 16, to be exact, that the circle was founded by Miss Frances Robie, now Mrs. John G. Morse III, a social welfare worker in Phippsburg, for the purpose of raising money to repair the chapel.

The first meeting was held in the Popham Library with Mrs. Laurence Taylor as Secretary pro-tem. After a discussion, the following ladies were elected to office: President, Mrs. Frank Scott: Vice President, Mrs. Ellison Moody, and Secretary-Treasurer, Mrs. Raymond Larrabee.

Driftwood from Popham Sands

It was not until the second meeting that the name Popham Circle was decided upon.

The first activity of the circle was a food sale, followed by a fair in the summer, thus giving the circle's treasury a balance of $125.

Over the years new members have taken the place of the old ones, but a membership of about seven has remained throughout the years.

As the schoolhouse was not in use in the fall of 1946, we asked the Superintendant of Schools, Mr. Stanwood G. Gilman, if we could have use of the building, and the School Board consented to this. It was there for the next few years that the circle carried on its various projects of suppers, entertainments, parties and fairs.

Outside of the large amount that has been spent on the chapel building, the circle, whenever the treasury of the church was low, carried on the regular duties of the parish by remembering the ill and shut-ins with cards, flowers, plants at Easter, also doing general charity work whenever necessary.

Later when the circle started using the library for its various projects, we were able to help out with a driveway and parking lot to be used jointly by the chapel and the library, besides helping with repairs on the library building.

Now that we have reached the twenty-five-year mark, we are not planning to sit back and reminisce over what we have done, instead we are presently at work on the project of helping the parish on the much-needed repairs to the chapel's steeple.

We have two honorary members, Mrs. Frank Scott, who worked with us right up to the time she had to leave her home due to ill health, and Mrs. Guy Crowley who, though not an active member now, still comes to our meetings whenever it is possible.

Florence Oliver

"Public Library, Popham Beach, ME."

Popham Library

At the turn of the century when Popham was in its hey day, its population was between eighty and a hundred people during the winter months. The village had a school attendance of between thirty and forty scholars.

The summer vacationers flocked to the hotels and cottages, and the whole place was alive with different activities the place afforded.

In August of 1907, through the efforts of several of the summer inhabitants, the subject of a library was brought to their attention. By August 1908, there was money enough raised through the donations and several social functions to start thinking of a site for the building.

A committee of three, namely Mrs. Thomas Percy, Mrs. Charles Marsh and E.H. Van Antwerp, was chosen to look into a site for the building. The site next to the chapel was finally chosen and conveyed in the summer of 1909 to the Association by the Shaw

Old roller skating rink at Popham Beach before 1910. In the forefront is the Hotel Rockledge's sewer pipe, supported above ground.

Lumber Co. and William T. Donnell. J. Arthur Stevens of Popham drew up the plans, and work was started that fall.

Uncle George and Uncle Lyman were the head builders and did the whole of the sheathing inside and the finish work.

Uncle Nat Perkins, a stone mason, built the stone fireplace from the sea-washed stones from Stage Island brought ashore by Guy Crowley, a member of the Coast Guard, and William Hodgkins.

Books were donated from various sources. A library association was formed, and Miss Lottie Stevens was hired as librarian, a job that she held for many years.

Over the years, the building remained pretty much the same except for a bathroom, which was added a few years ago.

In 1933 the Library Association was dissolved. It was unanimously voted to sell to the Beach Improvement Association all real and personal property, property rights and easements of the association, and they took the responsibility of the building. For a number of years the interest turned to improving the sidewalks, controlling the mosquitoes, etc., so the building was used mostly for social functions to raise money for these activities.

Many activities took place over the years to maintain interest among the young people, but times changed and they preferred to make their own entertainment, so planned events were eventually canceled.

The members of the Popham Circle were offered the use of the building, when not in use by the association. So, after the former schoolhouse, which we had been using, was put up for sale, we carried on our many activities of suppers, fairs, teas, Christmas entertainments and parties there.

Parking finally got to be a problem for both the library and the chapel. It was overcome by the parish and the Popham Associa-

The White Spot former Sea Grill 1900s.

Sea Grille run by Marguerite McNulty, later known as The White Spot. Photo by Ernest W. Oliver.

tion each giving enough land to build a driveway and parking lot between the two buildings for joint use.

In the last few years that I lived at Popham, there seemed to be some interest in the library among the summer residents, and several books by local authors were purchased. Children were especially interested in taking out the books.

In 1971, while Ernest Oliver was on the board of trustees, he received a letter from Mr. Ralph Gould of South Portland saying he had made a weathervane of the model of the *Virginia*, the first ship built in America in 1607. He made it purposely for some local building at Popham. The trustees were consulted and it was agreed to put it up on the library roof. Mr. Gould came over and erected the vane personally. Mr. Gould used to summer at Bay Point as a boy, and Popham was one of his favorite haunts.

Florence Oliver

Roller Skating Rink

The location in the photo above has been identified by two people as the old skating rink. It might have been at one time a part of the old icehouse. Mr. Edward P. Thomas Sr. said he had skated there, but he is the only one I have heard. At the time I received the picture, Uncle Lyme Oliver's eyesight wasn't good enough for him to identify it.

I asked Uncle George Oliver if he ever skated there, and he said he had a hard time keeping his feet on the ground without mounting himself on wheels.

Sea Grille or The White Spot

This is the Sea Grille on the south beach with Fox Island on the far right. This building originally sat on the west side of Silver Lake between the pond and the town road. Mrs. Marguerite McNulty bought it, moved it down to the beach, remodeled it for a restaurant and added a porch and bath houses.

It was known as the Sea Grille until it was sold to a Mr. White, who changed the name to White Spot.

There was a lot of activity around there, especially on a holiday and weekends. Marguerite had a piano and many a songfest was held.

During a bad storm in the [1960s], the sea washed out the bank and the White Spot broke into two pieces. It was beyond repair. The Phippsburg Fire Department finally came and burned it.

George Popham Club

There are probably not many people at Popham now that remember the George Popham Club. It was formed about 1911.

Driftwood from Popham Sands

Up to that time there was no organization that sponsored any social activities in the community. One annual event was a clam bake conducted each year under the leadership of Mr. Thomas Payne. It was at one of these bakes that a club was discussed and formed through the efforts of Mr. and Mrs. Payne and named George Popham Club. The twenty-ninth of August was set aside as George Popham Day, and every year a celebration was held.

This became one of the highlights of the summer. The steamer on the Bath run made an extra trip to bring passengers from Bath and along the route to Popham.

Tub, swimming and boat races were very popular with the young men and boys. Uncle Lyme Oliver's Kennebec Wherries were more than popular in the boat races.

At noon Rufus Lombard of West Bath put on the customary clam bake and many other delicacies were served at both hotels.

If the tide served, water sports could take place in the morning and a baseball game was held in the afternoon at the Ingraham Field (not Isaacsons).

For those not interested in some of these activities, the personnel at the Life Saving Station, later known as the Coast Guard Station, put on an exhibition of their activities. The breechers buoy and the Lyle life gun act was especially enjoyed by the men and boys.

A trip through Fort Popham and the lighthouse by the light keeper was always a popular treat.

The day usually ended with a dance at Society Hall, especially for those not able to take in the activities of the day. In those days, one had to know what he was doing when the announcer would call off a Hull's Victory, Chorus Jig, Lady of the Lake, Virginia Reel or a Boston Fancy.

By the time the old clock would point to midnight, everyone was willing to call it a day.

Florence Oliver

I was not acquainted with Popham in these times, but have heard of this through the family, who was always mixed up with them in some way.

There was always one man all the time I lived at Popham who upheld the tradition of George Popham Day as long as he was able, and that was Jimmy Heald of the Ashdale area. He could never understand why there was no activity on such an important day. After devouring several hot dogs, coffee, pie and ice cream at Spinney's store, he would journey home.

George Popham Day became extinct until a few years ago. The Popham Beach Association started to bring it alive again, but it could never be like the George Popham Day of old.

The following are from one of the old *Bath Times*:

> August 1917. The committee has decided to share fifty-fifty the proceeds with the Red Cross War Fund and a program which will furnish amusement during the day and evening, has been decided on. The U.S. soldiers stationed at the forts will assist by giving drills, camp pitching contests and other army sports. There will be land and water sports for girls and boys and men folks concluding in the evening by a pop concert and dance.

> August 23, 1914. Annual field day was one of the most successful in the organization's history. The first event was a series of drills by the life saving crew at Hunniwell's Beach Station under the direction of Captain Harvey Berry. Another interesting feature was the raising of a flag on the village school, a gift of Charles H. Hyde.
>
> The Ladies Sewing Circle was on hand with home cooked food, candy, cold drinks and homemade articles.

Driftwood from Popham Sands

Boats were available for anyone wanting to take a sail around the bay.

Clams and lobsters were available for those not wanting to go to the hotels to eat and the stores carried their usual stock of goodies.

The beach was lined with those wishing to enjoy a picnic lunch and a dip in the salt water. There was something for everyone to enjoy, and they did with great enthusiasm.

Chapter Five

Clam Industry

When one thinks of Popham Beach, the first thing that comes to mind is mosquitoes and then clams, or that is the way it used to be before the state declared the clams polluted. Somewhere I read once: "Popham mosquitoes are businesslike. They give you their bills and then they receipt themselves."

Today, clams are a luxury, but they used to be a cheap meal, especially when one could dig his own. When children want spending money today, they go and pick up bottles for the refund or baby sit, but in Ernest's day they would go and dig a mess of clams and peddle them around the beach to the cottage folks.

There was a special place that the children could dig even when they were young. It was called the Chowder Patch on the south side of the channel so no boat was needed. They were a nice size for steamers.

Once, when Ernest worked in one of the grocery stores, a crowd of girls rented a cottage for their vacation. They inquired of him where they could get some clams. He told them he would get some and deliver them to the cottage. After looking at them they asked him how to get them out of the shell. He asked them for a knife, but the only thing they could find was an old style can opener. He looked at it for a minute and then proceeded to get one shell opened and left them to enjoy their clams. I wonder if they might not have had steamed clams after all.

It was quite a sight when the tide was leaving the flats to see the diggers going off to dig. They would haul their boats up on the flats and dig out with the tide. The seagulls knew that when they saw the boats going, it meant a snack if they played it right. Often times a quick shower on a summer's day would take the clammers unawares and you would see them run to their skiffs and turn them part way over so they could get under to keep from getting wet. A good digger could dig a barrel a tide and up to two barrels. Arthur Moore used to be "king digger." When my daughters were small, they used to sell lemonade to the diggers as they came in and sing to them. The clammers would give them pennies for singing.

Trucks picked up the clammers at the head of the old government wharf at Fort Popham. Sometimes the clammers had to row the clams to Bay Point. Ernest said he had often dug a barrel and rowed them to Bay Point for two dollars a barrel. One winter they dug and shucked for fifty cents a gallon and had to pay the shipping costs, also the containers they shipped them in. One can hardly believe that today.

If one was choosey about the clams he wanted, no doubt he dug on the sand bar. These had nice large white shells but were not as plentiful as those dug in the mud. During the last of the digging, they were dug by a machine and went through a cleansing process. This did not last for long.

Cranberry Industry

One of the most important industries at Popham Beach in the early years was the growing of cranberries.

Popham Beach was divided between Charles Clark and Lyman

Florence Oliver

Oliver. In 1844, Mr. Oliver, taking the west side of the dividing line, went into farming and the growing of cranberries with John Marr. The state park is in that area today.

A sea wall was built to keep the water and debris out of the bogs and away from the vines. This was quite a task for all the vines had to be transplanted by hand. The one thing that was in their favor was the fact that there weren't as many people around in those days to trample on the vines. The wall lasted a good many years, but around 1918 the tides, caused by heavy winds, slowly swept it away and the meadows filled up with sand that choked out most of the vines.

When the berries started to get ripe and before the early fall frosts, the owners would hire pickers, mostly women, from the neighboring villages to harvest the crop. The meadows were all named so they could keep track of the harvesting. The ones that come to mind are Camp Meadow, West Meadow and Big Meadow.

After the berries were picked, they were hauled up to Mr. Oliver's house on the point and put into the cranberry house on the north shore of Atkins Bay. They were spread to ripen and dry on long tables and then winnowed to get out the stems, grass, leaves, before they were barreled for shipment.

Some years they shipped as many as three hundred barrels to Boston. There was always a market for them as they claimed they were a hardier berry than those of Cape Cod and kept longer. We still have the old stencil marked "Hunniwell's Point" that they used to mark the barrels.

In the days when fishing and trading were major industries, sea captains were as numerous as flies, as the old saying goes. When they loaded their ships for a long voyage, they would always include barrels of cranberries, stored in water, to prevent scurvy. Today it would be a matter of a supply of vitamins.

We, today, might look on it as an easy way to have made a living, but in those days without modern tools, it was a back-breaking job setting out and tending the vines in all kinds of weather.

Uncle Lyman said his father, Lyman Oliver, was so used up with rheumatism in his later years, from bending over and getting wet, that he couldn't stand up straight. After his death on October 10, 1887, his two sons, George and Lyman, kept the business going for a number of years.

Coal at Popham

The following are a few items from newspapers about 1919 or 1920:

> "It looks as though it was up to the people of Popham and Small Point to convince the Geological Society that there is a coal mine in that region by producing the mine."

Washington experts have failed to explain why coal at Popham comes ashore with three sides covered with barnacles, while the fourth side is clean and clear showing signs of cleavage from the main ledge or reef of coal.

People made it a practice to walk with Small Point and Popham Beaches in order to pick up the coal that was washed ashore. It was of the same quality one would get a few years ago when coal was the number one means of heating. It was free burning so it made excellent fuel.

I don't know what signs they had to convince them of coal in the area, but sometime as early as the 1830s, a crew of men with

Florence Oliver

Lyman Oliver as boss blower, blew for coal on the east side of Sabino Hill. The hole was predicted about forty feet deep—but alas, no coal! Uncle Lyme Oliver said he never asked his father if there were any other attempts to find coal. There are not many today that even know where the hole is. It was always referred to as "The Coal Hole." Over the years leaves and limbs off the trees have probably filled it in. The government fence around the property has protected anyone from finding it by mistake.

In the division deed of Popham Beach between Charles Clark and Lyman Oliver, it refers to "The Coal Hole."

Popham's Feldspar

Another industry at Popham, at least for a while, was the quarrying of feldspar. Sometime after the beginning of the 19th century, the J. W. Cummings Feldspar Co. leased a section of the John Marr farm, then known as Perkins, on Atkins Bay, from James

John Marr Farm on Atkins Bay. Later known as Perkins or Marsh. Demolished by the state of Maine, March 1971.

and Nathaniel Perkins. About forty men were set to work at once. Daily shipments were sent to Bath by scow to be ground at the company's plant at the South End.

Later Lyman I. Oliver and his son, Ernest, quarried some on their land near there. In order to do this, they had to buy a small piece of flats from the Perkins heirs to get a scow close enough to load it. It was said to be a good grade of feldspar although not a great amount of it.

Ice Business

When one can go the refrigerator and get a cold drink or something to cook that has been frozen indefinitely, he doesn't often think of the old days when ice had to be cut from the local ponds, stored in ice houses and covered with sawdust to keep it until the next winter.

Ice was a big industry in Phippsburg and Popham and played its part according to the old records. The *Bath Independent* gave a list of the ice tonnage for the year 1885, and Popham was listed at 30,000 tons.

An article from the *Maritime History of Maine* gives a good description of Yankee ingenuity: "The first shipment of Kennebec River ice took place around 1820. William Bradstreet came up the river in his ship *Orion* in the fall to Pittston, where she froze in at Dearborn's wharf. When the river broke up in the spring and the ice cakes floated about the brig, they were hauled aboard and stored in the hold. They sailed to Baltimore with a cargo that cost nothing and sold for eight hundred dollars."

From a newspaper clipping we find that the men were cutting ice from the Irving Pond (now Silver Lake) as early as 1850. A trestle work of 3080 feet in length ran from the pond down to

Florence Oliver

the shore on Atkins Bay where it was loaded onto vessels. This was taken down before 1880. I can remember some of the old posts at low tide when I went to Popham to live.

The following is an item from the *Bath Independent* 1882: "Messrs. Vickery and Glazier were at Popham the first of the week. The roof of the new icehouse is framed and ready to go up. The 1500 foot chute to the new wharf is nearly completed and a crew of about thirty-eight men are engaged. The machine purchased in Boston will be hauled down from Bath immediately by oxen. It will take two or three days to bring it down."

In December of 1883, 800 feet of the chute blew down and had to be replaced.

For a number of years, ice was cut in the pond and stored in the old icehouse by the side of Silver Lake. Elkaneh Wyman was the last one to peddle ice from there. Like everything else, when ice could be made by machinery, the business came to a standstill along the Kennebec River.

Chapter Six

Hotels

Popham Beach possibly became famous as a summer resort as far back as the 1800s. According to the *Lincoln Telegraph*, an old Bath newspaper, on March 25, 1836, is the following advertisement: "A Tavern to let" and signed by Samuel W. Look. In June of 1836, we find the old "Tavern" as Hunniwell's Point House. It sat about halfway on the left side of the ledge from the old entrance to the fort to the present Fort Popham. Uncle George Oliver told me it was a two story and half building with a basement, roofing, windows and a balcony around the first story. After viewing the drawings of the late Cyrus Longley displayed at the Phippsburg Museum, I am convinced he was right.

Excursions from Bath on the river steamers brought a lot of tourists for clam bakes and chowder parties, and soon more accommodations were needed.

Thomas Larry had a house on the ledge going into the fort, opposite what we call Larry's Rock today, where they fish. He accommodated folks occasionally. Soon boarding houses and hotels were springing up everywhere. At every change of ownership or in the construction of one, the building was renamed, so it is hard to make a distinction between them in a lot of cases.

Sometime in 1850, George Irving, a native of Scotland, bought

Florence Oliver

the old Shaw Mansion that sat on what today is the Isaacson's land. It contained seventeen rooms and overlooked Silver Lake and the ocean. It was considered to have one of the best views on the coast.

In 1878 Perkins and Stacey built the Riverside Hotel. It was considered one of the best along the coast. It contained forty-two rooms and was completely furnished. It opened in 1880 as the Eureka House.

About the same time the Ocean View House, known as the "pride of Popham," was being built about 150 feet above the ocean level on what was known as Seymour Bluff. In the fall of 1887 a western extension was built onto the original building. I believe that was the time it was named the "Rockledge." A better name couldn't have been selected.

A boardwalk ran down through the pines to the steps that went up to the hotel and folks would walk along to listen to the music that was played for dancing and singing during the evenings.

In 1885 Messrs. Perkins and Stacey built a hotel sixty feet by fifty feet, north of the Eureka House, known in later years as Fred Spinney's residence.

By this time Popham was in full swing with the Rockledge, Riverside, Eureka House and the Bayview run by Calvin Oliver, which was later the residence of Stanley Hyde.

The original ell of the house was moved there and the main house was built on afterwards.

Many new cottages had been built along the river beach and south beach, and by the turn of the century, it began to look as though Popham Beach would be a rival to Mount Desert.

About 1914 George Sinclair of Boston remodeled the old Spinney house on Long Island, across the Kennebec opposite Cox's Head, and made it into a fine bungalow for public use. It was named Croft Ledge. Ernest Oliver remembered when the river

Driftwood from Popham Sands

Riverside Hotel. Ralph Butler and Willard Rowe are in the boat.

"Small Point Harbor, ME. Alliquippa Hotel from the Harbor." From a postcard by Geo. S. Graves.

Florence Oliver

DW 117 S.H. Stacys Restaurant and Hotel, Popham Beach.

Ocean View House, Fort Popham.

Driftwood from Popham Sands

steamers would land there on a signal. .At that time it was called Sinclair's Boarding House.

Improvements at this time were being made to the Rockledge property. Timbers were cut from Popham woods to use in moving the main building to a new foundation. A big annex had been added, which included a music room. When finished it would have accommodated 200 guests and should have been ready for the 1915 season, but there is an old saying, "all good things come to an end" and such was the fate of the Rockledge, for on March of 1915, the worst fire up to that time took place on a Saturday afternoon caused by cinders from a smokestack of a saw mill on the shore of Silver Lake. A strong wind from the northeast soon caused it to get out of control. Only the six chimneys remained standing. Every available man, woman and child worked for hours removing furnishings from the hotel. Afterwards the things were sold and many a family had souvenirs of the Rockledge around their houses.

It was a great loss to the owners, but Colonel D.W. Wainwright of Boston Real Estate Trust still planned to go ahead with his plans of building a hotel on the same site. His plan was to include building bungalows on the cliff. The following is an article from a local newspaper: "Messrs. Dan Bishop and Lovejoy of Popham Beach have just concluded a deal with Messr. Rupert Les Erswell by which the Popham promoters became owners of the big casino building at Merrymeeting Park. The building will be torn down and the material removed by the owners."

According to the 1915 Brochure of the Rockledge, they evidently had had great plans for the hotel and I quote: "Summer season will formally open June 1st. And remain open to October 1st. And as much later as will warrant. A portion of the hotel will be open the entire year and special attractions will be offered to automobile parties, sportsmen, lovers of nature, and we promise to make you very comfortable in an informal way even in the dead of winter."

"Special Notice! It is earnestly requested that guests, when possible, notify the manager by mail or telephone when they expect to dine or sleep at the hotel in the winter months as this will ensure prompt service."

Nevertheless that was the end of the Rockledge and there are few around today who remember it.

In the meantime the Eureka House, by that time called the Riverside, had been enlarged to fifty rooms and was doing big business under the management of William Hamilton. A pavilion for a pool, billiard room and ice cream parlor was built on the front lawn.

By 1924 a lease on the hotel was taken by Mr. And Mrs. Fred Humiston formerly of the Aliquippa Hotel at Small Point Harbor. After a few years due to the increase of automobiles, there was a slacking in the hotel business and the place was sold by the town for taxes to Mr. And Mrs. Lawrence Taylor, who tore down and built a store, which they ran for a number of years. After they both had passed on, Ilene Percy leased it from their son, added a lunch room and is still in business at this writing.

Post Offices

Before the Civil War years, the roads were so bad that there was no regular mail delivery unless it came by steamer.

During the war years (1861-1865) Elbridge Oliver, a half brother to Uncle Lyme and Uncle George Oliver, was hired by the government to pick up the government mail at Parker's Head along with the village mail. When the tide served right he would walk

The first U.S. Post Office in Popham Beach, adjacent to the home of Ephram Marr. Mrs. Marr became its first postmaster in 1897. It was located across from Popham Chapel. From a postcard by Geo. S. Graves.

Postmaster Marguerite Irving McNutty.

Florence Oliver

across the flats to Malcolm's Cove, later Ed De Berry's property, and walk the rest of the way by the town road.

Later, as the roads improved, a trip overland by stage was due in at noon every day, also one trip by steamer in the winter months, and two in the summer. Mail service was as good if not better than in the city. Timmy Small was one of the old stage drivers, also William "Bill" S. Oliver, of Small Point. This was a bad route due to the big marsh with its drifting snow and the high tides. Often when he was very late due to the roads, he would bunk in with his horse in the old stable behind Uncle Nat Perkins' house (now Minot Percy's).

James M. Perkins was postmaster in 1888 and conducted the office in the Perkins and Stacey store.

In 1897, Ephraim Marr was appointed postmaster at Popham and the office was moved to the Haley and Marr store. Later he moved an old building alongside of his house, across the street from the chapel, and made it into a post office, the first at Popham Beach.

An item in a local newspaper states: "In 1915 E.S. Marr, postmaster at Popham Beach received notice from Washington of his being retained as postmaster under the executive orders of May 7, 1914." Mr. Marr has been postmaster at Popham since 1897 and the news of his appointment is pleasant for his many friends."

On January 26, 1925, Marguerite McNulty was commissioned

Previous page lower left: *Postmaster Marguerite Irving McNulty retired August 31, 1960, after more than 30 years of service. On August 29, grateful friends and postal patrons presented her with a sterling silver Revere bowl, a purse of silver dollars, and a bouquet of flowers. Pictured with her are the children of summer residents Stephen Norris and Katy Phialas, who presented McNulty with the gifts.*

to the office as postmistress. She bought the building used by Mr. Marr and moved it across the street next to the library. Her husband, Ed McNulty, conducted a small store along with the post office. After Ed died she remodeled it and moved there to live and conduct the post office. After the war years, in the [1940s] forties, Marguerite bought the former Nat Perkins place and operated the post office in the winter store of Fred H. Spinney located in the north end of his house, until he remodeled the house to make more rooms for tourists.

In 1956 Marguerite moved into her newly built post office she had built by Ernest W. Oliver at the rear of her house. She remained as postmistress until her retirement on August 30, 1960, after thirty-five years of duty.

After Marguerite's retirement, Thelma Chambers of the Ashdale district bought the building from Marguerite and carried on as postmistress for a while. Later she moved the building down nearer the Coast Guard Station. Later it was bought for use as a cottage. Helen Gagnon had the route most of the time that I lived at Popham, and there never was a more faithful mail carrier. I've known her to walk and carry the mail, when she got stuck, for miles to get the first class mail to the office.

The 350th anniversary of the Popham Colony occurred in 1957 while Marguerite McNulty was in the post office. After reconsidering, on request, Postmaster General Summerfield issued a special stamp commemorating the 350th anniversary of the building of the Virginia of Sagadahock at the Popham Colony in 1607. It was supposed to be the first ship built in America. The First Day Issue of the stamp was to be at Bath during the Popham Colony celebration that was to be held there.

A good many people thought it was too bad that Popham couldn't have the honor of having the first sale of the stamps, it being the anniversary of the colony.

Mr. Lawrence Taylor, who ran the store on the property of the old Riverside Hotel decided "Where there is a will, there is a way," and came up with an idea. He notified everyone that he saw and could get in touch with to order what stamps they wanted by the evening of August 14th and to be ready by ten o'clock the next morning to pick them up. He went to Bath and purchased the stamps as soon as he could get into the office, lost no time in getting to Popham where he distributed them in time to get them directed and in the mail before it left that day.

Although they couldn't be marked as First Day Covers, they contained the postmark of Popham Beach. Stamp enthusiasts have made the remark that envelopes and cards postmarked Popham Beach will someday be worth more that those postmarked Bath, considering the design on the stamp was commemorating the ship *Virginia* of the Popham Colony.

Mrs. Etta Taylor took over the post office after Thelma Chambers. They built a piece onto their store, and it remained as a post office long after both Mr. and Mrs. Taylor had passed away. It eventually became a rural station.

Country or General Stores

Stores played a big part in the lives of the people years ago at Popham Beach. It was there that the people met their neighbors to talk over the topics of the day, politics, get the mail and meet the newcomers at to Popham Beach.

For years there were two stores, Haley & Marr and Perkins & Stacey, later Oliver & Myers and L. J. Oliver. Later the Spinney's from Bay Point came over and ran a store.

In 1939, when I went to Popham to live, Ernest Spinney was

Driftwood from Popham Sands

running a small store on the edge of the beach approximately where the restaurant sits today. In the winter he carried on a small store in a room of the house. Sometime in the [1940s]'forties, the store was washed out in a bad storm, and later Fred H. Spinney, his son, built the present store. He also took the room on the north side of the house for a winter store and rented a room to Marguerite McNulty for the post office.

Sometime in the [1950s]fifties, Mr. and Mrs. Laurence Taylor bought the old Riverside Hotel property for taxes from the town and ran a store and later the post office.

When spring arrived, the grocery stores were more or less treated like the homes, an annual cleanup would be in progress getting ready for the summer trade. A fresh coat of paint and the shelves were newly stocked and the place would take on a new look.

An old country store carried about everything one would need in a home for folks who didn't go to Bath every other day for shopping. If some of the younger folks could go into one of the old stores, they wouldn't know what to do. One didn't go and pick up what they wanted, you had to be waited on for most things, coffee had to be ground and weighed. Sugar, dry beans, crackers and cookies and even peanut butter had to be measured out and weighed.. There were few bags in the earlier years. Everything was done up in a piece of wrapping paper. It was a work of art to do sugar, etc., in a piece of paper without spilling it on the way home.

Ernest used to tell about a boy who came to the store for some molasses and had forgotten to bring the jug. Mr. Stacy, the storekeeper, said he could help him if he was going right home. He put the molasses in a paper bag and told the boy to be sure and not set the bag down until he got home. I wouldn't recommend it to everyone. Molasses had to be cranked out of a barrel, and

Florence Oliver

Oliver & Myers Groceries. Standing: Walter Morrison. Sitting: Leroy Myers and Lyman I. Oliver.

E. S. Marr Store and post office beside his house across from library, Popham Beach. L-R: Katherine Perkins, Florence Chandler, Jane Stevens, Ellen Stevens, Hiram Stevens, ? Spinney, Anna Perkins, Bob Stevens behind carriage. 1920.

L.J. Oliver Store. L-R: Lyman I. Oliver, Louie Oliver, George Oliver.

in the winter it was an endless chore—so the old saying "slow as cold molasses."

There was always a bunch of bananas hung up in the store in the summertime, and that was a welcome sight. The stores couldn't carry them in the winter. There was always a small narrow-edged knife with a rounded blade to cut the bananas from the stalk. I can remember buying the bananas for a nickel apiece.

Tea bags hadn't been invented. Tea came in tins. There were names like Pekoe, Orange Pekoe, Oolong and Formosa that come to my mind.

A cheese came in a round wooden box about fifteen inches or so across. It was cut like a layer cake (in wedges) and wrapped in a piece of paper. I don't remember any of the varieties—just the kind the old folks called "rat bait."

A barrel of salt pork was a "must" in the old country store. Everyone used pork for frying. There was no Crisco or cooking spray. Women used lard and oleomargarine for cooking. Sometimes it would take more than one attempt at spearing the pork to get just the right piece for those Saturday night beans. A piece with a streak of lean meat was mostly preferred.

Mrs. Hiram Stevens, who lived next to the chapel, used to bake beans and steam brown bread on Saturdays to sell. On occasion Ernest said his folks used to indulge once in a while. Mrs. Stevens used to bake raised bread, too, and she could tell just how many loaves she could get out of a barrel of flour.

In most of the stores there was a closed cabinet where all the "medicine" was kept. This consisted of oils of wintergreen and peppermint, cloves and cinnamon, not forgetting Jamaican ginger. There were ointments and salves for aching joints after clamming and mosquito bites. Toothache gum and drops were a must, also patent cough medicine and Smith Brothers cough drops with the licorice flavoring. Then there were the laxatives—with castor oil right out front, nitre for fever and paregoric for the stomach—all without a prescription.

Tinware and yard goods were usually found at the rear of the store. Baking pans, dippers, muffin pans, water pails, wash tubs, tea kettles, dinner pails, coffee pots, wash basins, dish pans, flour sieves, wash boards, mops and brooms were among the things you would find. Yard goods were usually unbleached muslin, ginghams, calicoes and cotton prints, not forgetting the mosquito netting they used to tack onto the window casing and the oilcloth for the kitchen table.

Fresh salmon and peas were a treat for Fourth of July. There were several weirs and hedges along the bay and the river, and smoked shad and herring were stocked for winter use.

Probably one of the most popular spots in the store was the candy counter. The Spinneys were always great for a lot of candy. They said there was a lot of profit in it in those days. Penny candy was in great demand as nickels and dimes were not too easy to come by. There were all-day suckers in many flavors, jaw breakers, needhams, coconut balls, gum, peppermints and checkerberry drops, lozenges, and wafers, licorice sticks, the old fashioned chocolate drops and others too numerous to mention. The candy bags came in colored stripes of green, yellow, pink and purple, and for five cents, if one shopped carefully, he could come out of the store with a bag nearly full.

Chocolates were bought in half and pound boxes or could be bought loose. Ernest could tell the flavor of chocolate by the design on the top of it.

Few cigarettes were seen. Most men smoked a pipe or cigars and some chewed tobacco that came in packages or plugs. Cigars could be bought singularly or in packages or boxes. In one of the stores there was a machine in the shape of a Native American. It sat on the counter with the tobacco. If a man wanted to smoke a cigar he would press the end of the cigar, into the machine where a sharp blade would cut it off. Many a curious child would try the same with his finger only to find out his mistake.

Since there was no electricity, soda pop or tonic was kept in an open cooler on chunks of ice. Some of the most popular were ginger ale, Moxie, root and birch beer, sarsaparilla, cream soda, strawberry and lemon-lime, all for five cents except for the Moxie, which came only in large bottles for a quarter.

A delivery wagon made two trips a day around the beach. The morning trip would be to take the orders, as there were few telephones then. In the afternoon the wagoneer would deliver the orders. There was no particular road in some places on the beach; the wagons went anywhere a horse could go.

It was common to see a person coming or going to the store carrying a kerosene can. Houses were lit by lamps and the oil companies did not peddle from door to door. The cans came in different sizes; some were a gallon size, some two gallons up to five gallons. I can remember a man coming to the store with his can and the storekeeper putting a small potato over the spout so it wouldn't spill over in his wagon. Ordinarily the large cans had a cover for the spout as well as the top.

The stores burned coal to keep things from freezing. The stoves were the old pot-bellied type, and they were nice to sit around and warm your feet.

Men folks whiled away many an hour in the old stores waiting for the arrival of the mail, talking over the events of the day, the weather, etc. In early spring Town Meeting was a big topic of these store get-togethers. Everyone spoke his piece and tempers were apt to clash. It was like the old saying:

"Everyone does a lot of talking about the weather, but nobody does anything about it."

Popham Schoolhouses

The first mention of a school that I can find at Hunniwell's Point is in November of 1835, when G.W. Richardson was paid to board the school mistress and hire for the school room. Hunniwell's Point was number four in the district. There were thirty-two pupils. This seems like a large school for the size of the community at the time, but remember it took only two or three families to come up with that number of children in those days.

School was held in the various homes and in the old stone barracks at the old fort, which was taken down when the present fort was built. Uncle George Oliver started school in a room of his father's house about 1858. The teacher came down pretty hard on discipline. On his first day of school, Uncle George fled from the room, to be found standing in the fireplace of what was called the Borning Room.

The room where school was kept was off the old kitchen in what was called in those days the inner shed, where they washed clothes, etc. The floor was lower than the kitchen floor, making a step or so into the shed. Years afterwards when they did some remodeling, the kitchen was put out in this shed and the floor was raised to the same level as the main house. One day, as I was washing the floor, I made the remark to Uncle Lyman Oliver, George's brother, that the door sill was worn in rather a peculiar manner. He told me that was George's seat when he went there to school. By the looks of the sill, I got the idea that Uncle George didn't sit too quiet when he went to school.

Uncle Lyme told of a hardwood ruler that the teacher had when he went to school. I don't know how he knew it was hard unless he

Florence Oliver

had the experience of feeling it. Those were the days when "sparing the rod" weren't thought of.

Sometime after the Civil War the ladies of the village decided a schoolhouse was needed, so they took up a subscription, and with the various ways of making money in those days, they got a schoolhouse. Lyman Oliver, father of Uncle George and Uncle Lyme, provided a piece of land for building the house as long as it continued to be used as a school.

The town report of 1894 mentioned a free high school donation. I think Uncle George's son Earl went to that, for I have seen books in our house at Popham that belonged to him. He had taken double-entry bookkeeping, algebra, English literature and subjects he wouldn't have taken in a regular town school.

In the 1902 town report, $800 was appropriated for a new schoolhouse. By that time the population had outgrown the old schoolhouse. The cost was $800.62. The lot for this building was taken off the deed of Frank Oliver, now Mrs. Mildred Sprague's.

Country schools were very much different than the grade schools of the city. Children of all ages from five on up through twenty and older were taught in one room by one teacher. This probably sounds confusing, but both the teachers and scholars were used to this way of teaching.

The pupils weren't even graded. They recited in groups that met with their achievement. A number of classes such as spelling and reading were oral, but many classes were written, giving the teacher time for the slower learners. Some of the older scholars and boys went to school only during the winter months when they were not needed to work on the farms, etc. The younger pupils learned considerably from listening to the teachers talk to the older pupils.

Teachers usually boarded with the parents of the children for a couple of weeks at a time.

Popham Beach School circa 1905. Ernest Oliver in back row left side wearing cap.

About 1903, the selectmen of the town, Charles Minot, William N. Beal and Winfield W. Morse, sold the old school building to Ephraim Marr for the consideration of $11, that being the highest bid at an auction held on the site of the building, September 12, 1903. The deed was dated February 23, 1904. Soon after obtaining the building, Mr. Marr, rather than moving it, sold it to Uncle Lyme Oliver, where he built many a boat there until he sold the land and building to Clarence Perkins, who repaired it and made himself a home.

In 1918 to 1920, the school was closed for a lack of pupils. What few there were went to Phippsburg Center or Percy District by the mail steamer. School was maintained in this building until

Florence Oliver

about 1946 or so when scholars numbered fewer than six. These were transported to Small Point for a short time.

After the Consolidated School was built and the town decided to sell all the old schoolhouses, Popham School was the first one up for bid. Mr. Norman Markham, a contractor, bought the building and used it for a shop. Later it was sold for use as a summer cottage.

Chapter Seven

"The Basin" Phippsburg, Maine

Written by Mrs. Ernest W. Oliver at the time the Phippsburg Historical Society was collecting information from the various parts of the town to put into a book later known as Phippsburg Fair to the Wind.

To really appreciate The Basin, one should enter it by the narrows on the New Meadows by boat and explore its interesting coves and shoreline. But as this is not always convenient, we must lay our course over the narrow country road that winds around the banks

"The Basin," in Sebasco, Maine. Photo by Geo. S. Graves.

Florence Oliver

William Butler's homestead at "The Basin" in Sebasco.

that overlook the circular bowl from whence it received its name.

Almost every cove and point on the basin has its story to tell, and in many instances it is our history of today. The eastern shore of the New Meadows River was settled long before the western shore of the Kennebec except for the Popham settlement of 1607.

Starting where the road leaves to go to the old Mica Mine, we journey down along the newly repaired road towards the lower Basin area. Passing Falls Cove, there is a long hill known as Batchelder's Hill, where the late Captain Batchelder lived and where the road runs close to the shore. If one should take the time to inspect this point of land, he would see the old ringbolts still in the ledges on the shore and on another ledge a few feet away, and running parallel to this one, forming a sort of cradle where it is possible a schooner of some sort was built at one time.

An interesting bit of history refers to a vessel built in The Basin before the French and Indian War. During that contest, the vessel was captured by the French. It is said that the French paid for the capture in the large indemnity they paid to this government, but the heirs of Mr. Mereen, the owner and the builder, and the first dweller on what is more widely known as Brightwater, never received the money due them, for the technical reason that one document called the vessel a "bark," and another a "ship."

At the bend of the next cove we find the house of Captain George Rogers of the ill-fated ship the *Hanover*, which was wrecked off Pond Island in 1849 as she missed her stays in trying to enter the river in a storm. This was also the home of Chester Oliver, one of Phippsburg's native ministers, who was the grandson of the late Captain Joseph Perry. In an adjoining cove, called Perry's Cove, we find a steam sawmill that dates back to the 1700s. From an old deed dated March 9, 1801, from Timothy Batchelder: "This gives us to understand that several families had a hand in this industry. The remains of the old dam are still visible."

The Perry farm had been owned by the Perrys since 1721, perhaps longer, and comprised more than 300 acres. This farm was later broken up into several farms, the last Perry farm being that of James C. Perry, father of the late Mrs. Annie Perry Pease, and more recently owned by the O'Callaghans.

Here the road separates to join again farther down in The Basin where we find the old schoolhouse and the Lower chapel. Keeping to the right we go up what is known as Long Hill where on the hillside known as Spaulding Field we find the William Perry Cemetery. At the top of the hill we find another of our oldest farms, that of Eli Batchelder, later known as William Butler's and presently owned by one of our former selectmen, Mark Harrington. The old Batchelder graveyard can still be seen on the premises.

In 1884, a group of interested people formed The Basin Benevolent Association for the purpose of erecting a chapel. Land was procured from John Perry by the trustees, and it was stipulated that the land was not to be used for any purpose except for the erection

Florence Oliver

Mill at "The Basin," Sebasco, Maine.

of a chapel. A chapel was erected about 1886 and was known as the Lower chapel, or Valley chapel, having been built at the foot of the hill leading to Bartlett's store and next to the schoolhouse.

For some time need was felt of a church organization, so after a successful summer session of religious work in 1892, carried on by a student from Bangor Seminary in the Valley or Lower chapel, it was decided to form a branch of the Congregational Church at Phippsburg Center. Several members were received into membership by confession of faith by letter and one from the Lutheran Church. It is expected that this did not work out too well, as in 1893 an article in a local newspaper spoke of church robbery in one of the local churches. Some of the old, well-meaning members of the church, to which the branch was united, said they did not think it was just right to pilfer from another church, so the matter was dropped.

We pick up the Lower chapel again in 1906 in the town report states that the Lower chapel was a branch of the Small Point Church but not generally occupied. Unfortunately, the chapel, which was valued at $1500, burned in a raging forest fire in the 1920s in the month of August, but the schoolhouse built in 1897 was saved.

Another chapel, built about the same time and known as the Upper chapel was erected at the top of the hill on the new road to Bartlett's store running westerly from the schoolhouse and near the old Bartlett homestead. The Upper Chapel was occupied by a Hellenise Society. It was used by the Nazarenes until 1958, when they bought the old schoolhouse from the town and converted it into a church. The old Upper chapel still stands unoccupied.

The area wouldn't be complete without mention of the well-known Malaga Island located in Casco Bay off the westerly shore of The Basin. The island contains about sixty acres and was occupied for many years by a colony of residents who had received considerable notoriety on their mode of living. December 1912 saw the disintegration of the colony that for years had been their home. Governor Plaisted said that the state of Maine owed it to the inhabitants to give them better moral possibilities.

The Island was purchased for $400 plus expenses from the Perry heirs, Scott Perry having been authorized to represent them. Afterwards the State sold it at bid, the bids ranging from $150 to $1650. It was sold to Dr. E.A. Wilson of Belfast for $1650.

It was not until 1896, when the new post office was established at The Basin, that this area became known as Sebasco. Most of the residents of the north side of The Basin repudiated the post office as well as the name they used—Basco. Even today, those that had any close connections with this area, still call it The Basin.

Florence Oliver

Kennebec River

Fair Kennebec, still art thou dear,
Though far my wandering feet have strayed.
And time has garnered many a year
Since on thy banks a child I played.
What is the storied Rhine to thee,
With castled crag and vine-clad hill?
Unmoved its glory I can see;
But thine, remembered, thrills me still.
What cliff can match thy beetling ledge,
O'er which my young eyes peered with awe
And fancied, leaping from its edge,
The hunted Indian still they saw?
What ancient castle can compare
With that gray, riven rock of thine,
Which oft we boys with sword in air
Assailed in mimic battle line.
What haunted dragon's den of yere
Can waken that mysterious dread,
With which I gazed the wild waves o'er,
At thy grim cave no foot might tread?
Deep in my heart the charm I feel
That grand Niagara wields o'er all;
But fonder memories o'er me steal
When fancy hears thy waters fall.
Thy deep voice lulled my childhood's sleep
When life was dawning fair and bright,
And still its tones their magic keep
Though fast my day glooms into night.

Driftwood from Popham Sands

Thy gleaming waves no rivals knew;
At times they sparkle in my heart
At times I see, their depths below,
A new world into being start;
When autumn skies and forests gay
Lie spread beneath thy glassy sheen
Unmoved from earth I drift away
In dreamy bliss the heavens between.
Ah! Nevermore can I untwine
The cords that bind my heart to thee;
The glorious gifts that once were thine
I find no more on land or sea.

—A.W. Gould, *Portland Transcript*

Chaper Eight

Remembrance

Christmas Poems by Florence Reed Oliver

Each year at Christmas time money was too dear to spend on store-bought Christmas cards. Florence Oliver wrote poetry and sent her greetings for the holidays to friends and neighbors.

1970

Christmas time is here again
And gifts must be selected for all our kin.
The hustle and bustle we all bear with joy
While gifts we select of games and toys.
The letters to Santa are on their way
And everything's set for the coming day.
Grandma watches TV as she rests weary feet
And Grandpa sits near and really looks beat.
But a Merry Xmas from all at this joint.
Your friends "The Olivers" on Horse Ketch Point.

Driftwood from Popham Sands

Christmas Greetings from Popham Beach, 1903.

1975

The seasons come, the seasons go
And the frosty mornings remind one of snow.
The children are bundled up ready for play
In mismated mitts from last Christmas' gifts.
Comic books are put aside for catalogues from far and wide.
Each night a new list is brought to attention
Of books, games and toys—too numerous to mention.
There is plenty of time one says to himself,
The Halloween costumes have just left the shelf.
But over the years we've learned it doesn't pay to wait,
It's better to buy early—than get there too late.
Grandma marks off the days as they pass
For she will be spending Xmas in Mass.

Florence Oliver

1978

As usual at this time of year
My head is tired as can be.
So I've drawn a mental blank
Which is not unusual for me.
However, I would like to take this opportunity
To wish you a Happy Xmas Day
And the New Year that's on it way.
I think we poor old Grandmas
Who strive so hard to remember
Do very, very well indeed
To survive clear through December!

Undated

As we greet the holiday season
In a joyful, happy way
Our wishes go to your home
For a merry Christmas Day.
The busy throng of shoppers
Go merrily to and fro
Wishing all a Merry Christmas
With happy hearts aglow.
At home the tree is set and trimmed
The doorway wreath is hung
Now everyone is waiting
For the Carols to be sung.
Last will be the stockings
All hanging in a row.

Driftwood from Popham Sands

Then Grandmama and Mother
Off to bed will go.
The clock is striking midnight
And it's time for Old St. Nickolas
As they lock the door and shut off the lights
They turn to say, "Merry Christmas."

Florence and Ernest Oliver, Christmas 1962, at the home of her brother, Robert Reed, in Waldoboro, Maine.

Bits & Pieces

Oliver
Family Tree
Maine

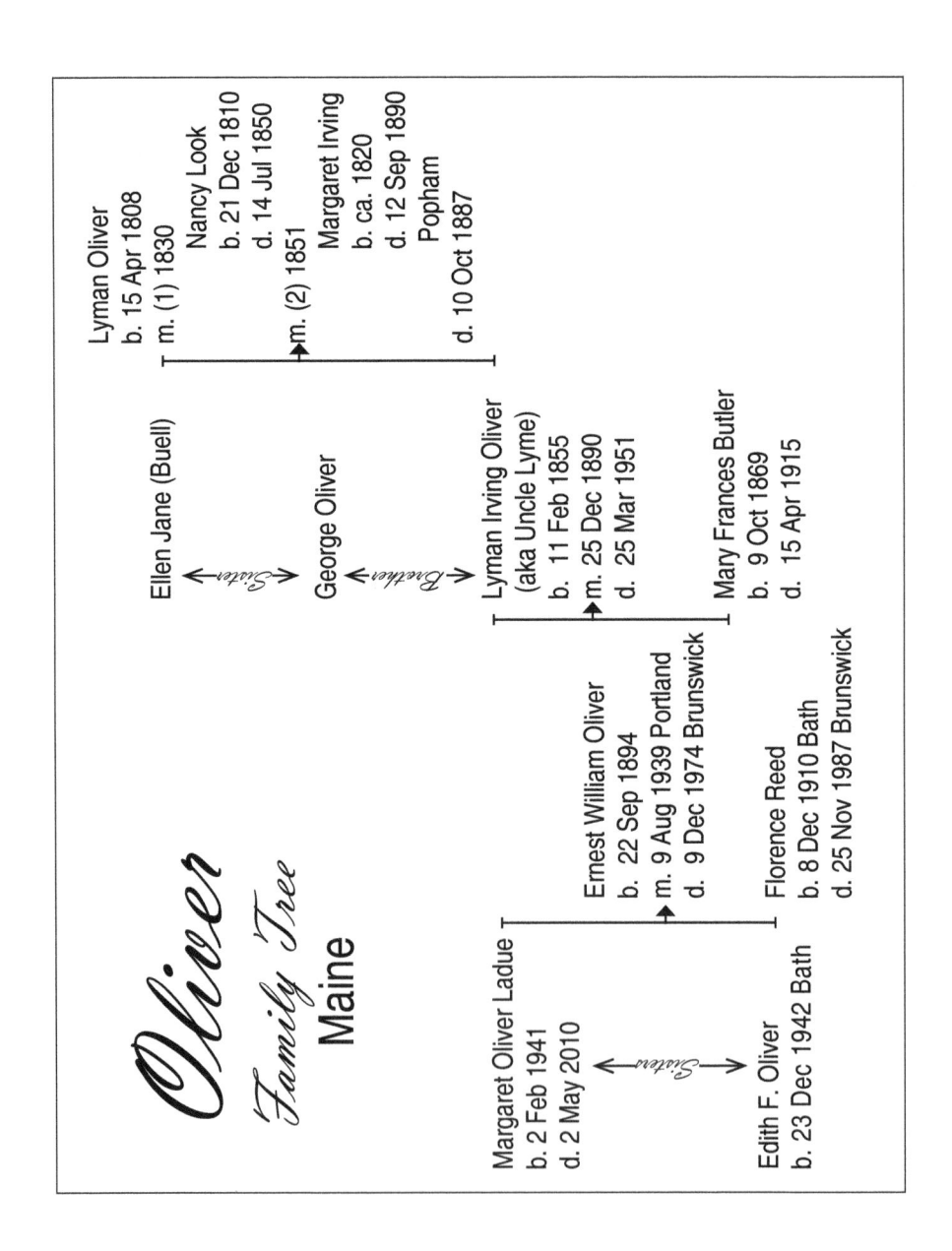

Lyman Oliver
b. 15 Apr 1808
m. (1) 1830
    Nancy Look
    b. 21 Dec 1810
    d. 14 Jul 1850
m. (2) 1851
    Margaret Irving
    b. ca. 1820
    d. 12 Sep 1890 Popham
d. 10 Oct 1887

Ellen Jane (Buell) ←*Sister*→ George Oliver ←*Brother*→ Lyman Irving Oliver (aka Uncle Lyme)
b. 11 Feb 1855
m. 25 Dec 1890
d. 25 Mar 1951

Mary Frances Butler
b. 9 Oct 1869
d. 15 Apr 1915

Ernest William Oliver
b. 22 Sep 1894
m. 9 Aug 1939 Portland
d. 9 Dec 1974 Brunswick

Florence Reed
b. 8 Dec 1910 Bath
d. 25 Nov 1987 Brunswick

Margaret Oliver Ladue
b. 2 Feb 1941
d. 2 May 2010

←*Sister*→

Edith F. Oliver
b. 23 Dec 1942 Bath

150

Resources

As mentioned in Note to Readers, this book has no citations. The publisher offers here a list of sources—some were used and some might have been used by the author, now deceased. This list is to help those who wish to conduct further research on any of the topics contained in this book.

Owen, Henry Wilson. T*he Edward Clarence Plummer History of Bath.* Bath, Maine: Bath Area Bicentennial Committee, 1976.

Phippsburg Historical Society. *Phippsburg Fair to the Wind.* Lewiston, ME: Phippsburg Historical Society, 1976.

Reed, Parker McCobb. *History of Bath and Environs, Sagadahoc County, Maine: 1607-1894.* Portland, ME: Lakdeside Press, Printers, 1894.

Sewall, Rufus King. *Ancient Dominion of Maine.* Boston, MA: Elisha Clark Company, 1859.

Stevens, James E Perkins & Jane. *One Man's World: Popham Beach, Maine.* Freeport, ME: The Bond Wheelright Company, 1974.

Thayer, Henry Otis. *The Sagadahoc Colony, comprising the relation of a voyage into New England.* Portland, ME: Gorges Society, 1892.

Various deeds in the Sagadahoc Registry of Deeds, Bath, ME.

Also, personal papers of Florence Oliver held by Edith Oliver comprised of clippings from *Bath Independent, Bath Times, Lincoln Telegraph, Phippsburg Observer, Portland Transcript, Times Dispatch,* brochures, posters and advertising pamphlets.

Edith Oliver and Margaret Oliver Ladue at Oliver home.

Florence Oliver

Ernest W. Oliver in uniform. He was the husband of the author, Florence Oliver, and father of Edith and Margaret.

Rune stone on Oliver property.

Above: Ernest W. Oliver, 78 years old, sitting on a covering he made for rune stone in 1972. Right: Lyman I. Oliver points to the rune stone with his cane.

154

Florence Reed Oliver
1910-1987

Florence Reed Oliver was born in Bath, Maine, on December 8, 1910, and grew up in Day's Ferry, Woolwich, Maine. She attended grade school in Day's Ferry and graduated from Morse High School in Bath in 1928. She later graduated from Gorham Normal School and taught school in Phippsburg while boarding with Eleanor and Edward Thomas in Cox's Head. She married Ernest Oliver in 1939 and raised two daughters, Margaret and Edith, at Popham. Florence was active in many organizations in Phippsburg, including the Daughters of the American Revolution, Phippsburg Historical Society, Unity Circle and Popham Circle. She was a member of the Small Point Church and an organist at the Popham Chapel. Florence was a contributor to the *Bath Independent* newspaper and a field researcher and contributor to the historical book written by the Phippsburg Historical Society, *Phippsburg Fair to the Wind,* published in 1964.

She moved to Bath after the death of her husband, Ernest W. Oliver. Florence passed away November 25, 1987.